UNLIKE A BOSS

Positive People Leadership Skills

You Wish Your Manager Had

ALEXANDER N. ANDREWS

Published by Lulu Publishing & Limelight Publishing, 2022

ISBN 978-1-4717-3275-1

Cover design by Lynette Greenfield @ Limelight Publishing.

Image and quote of Kisean Paul Anderson (Sean Kingston), supplied by Lynette Greenfield @ Limelight Publishing
info@limelightpublishing.com

limelightpublishing.com
lulu.com

CONTENTS

A shout out to the small handful of leaders who were positive examples to me in my career, and to the many bosses who weren't - you have each inspired me in different ways to truly place people at the centre of my leadership approach.

Most importantly, I dedicate this book to my beautiful wife and children. They inspire me every day to do what I do and have endured many an absence from me when work took me away. You are why a balanced work and home life for me is so important! I love you all very much.

BE A PEOPLE LEADER, NOT JUST A MANAGER

I'll put it out there. A lot of people leaders are terrible at being people leaders; they're the boss. A controversial statement, I suspect, but true nonetheless. No matter your generation or country of origin, you will have come across a leader, and often more than one in your career (as is the case with me), that has little idea how to lead people or does not care about the impact of their leadership style.

Some of these people may have delivered quick results for whoever gave them this responsibility, but what was the toll it took on the people they led? Did these leaders leave a trail of destruction in their wake? Were the results they achieved sustainable? Or was it simply a matter of them blowing in like a cyclone, creating chaos, generating a few short-term financial wins, and then blowing out, only for others to see the quick gains collapse just as quickly?

It's a sad indictment on the leaders I have worked with throughout my career, which spans three decades, that I have learnt more from them about what **not** to do than what to do. Thankfully, there were a few exceptions. For example, very early in my career,

1

I was fortunate to work for a leader who gave me extra responsibilities outside of my day job to test the spark he saw in me. I was able to deliver results in that project beyond his expectations, and as a result, he gave me my first real break in a leadership role. He did this not because I was the best technically—I actually knew very little about the area he asked me to lead—but because he liked what he saw in my leadership style. He took a punt on me. So, I have him to thank for getting me off to a great start. From that defining moment in my career—with the welcome addition of the time he took to coach me and further supported by various leadership courses—I was determined to *pay it forward* by looking for the spark in people to help them grow.

I left the relative sanctuary of that workplace after a promotion within the organisation. In the years that followed, I was to see and experience a variety of leadership styles. Some of the leaders I worked for were terrific at what they did; I just wasn't inspired to emulate their leadership style. A common trait was that they were self-absorbed. OK, that's a generalisation as there were some good eggs amongst them. Others truly sucked—to call them leaders would do leadership a grave disservice. They were, at best, managers—maintainers of things, some of which happened to be people. These people and the trail of destruction they left behind and, in some cases, more subtle negatives have given me the gift of fodder for this book, for which I am grateful. There's that well-used saying, *we learn from our mistakes*, and while that is very powerful, I also believe we can learn from the mistakes of others.

I am a glass-half-full kind of guy who tries to take a positive from most situations. The positive I took from some of the less-than-illustrious managers I have worked for has been to use their poor leadership traits as lessons on how not to behave myself as a leader—that is, I learnt from their mistakes. Often these leaders would be shocked to receive employee engagement survey results highlighting a lack of engagement in their departments/divisions. Then they would proceed to discount the qualitative feedback in black and white before their very eyes: "I'm not like that", "No, that's just one person's view". Some might set out with good intentions to action improvement initiatives aimed at making the result better next year. But these efforts were like spray painting a rusty car; the rust always comes back. In focusing on achieving a better engagement survey result, they were focusing on the wrong thing. Generally, their action plans consisted of short-term, sugar-boost initiatives that gave a temporary high. Instead, the focus should have been on addressing the fundamentals, and that starts at the top: How are we leading? What is the environment we are creating for our team members? What is my leadership shadow (remembering that we, as leaders, set the tone)?

My own style of leadership is to put people first. Now, you might ask what that means. It means actively listening to the members of my team and, importantly, creating opportunities to engage with them. So, in the example above, in response to engagement surveys, I like to run focus groups to really get to the crux of the matter. I am fortunate to have had a good track record of creating highly engaged work environments, reflected in the scores achieved in such engagement surveys. Even so, there is always much to learn from this sort of feedback. While a trait of many leaders I have worked with, arrogance is a significant pitfall of successful leadership. We can always learn, and those learnings often come from our team. Listening intently, I believe, is critical to the success of any leader.

> When I talk to managers, I get the feeling that they
> are important. When I talk to leaders, I get the
> feeling that I am important.
>
> *-Alexander den Heijer*

One of the world's most successful entrepreneurs/business leaders is Sir Richard Branson. Sir Richard has a simple philosophy: *put the team first*. This is not some fad that will go away, nor is it some trick to get the best out of people by manipulating them into thinking they're important. Frankly, I have zero tolerance for that kind of behaviour. People also aren't stupid; most can see right through that sort of conduct. At the risk of being taken for a kook, I'll go as far as to say this. Just as you would hope people who set out to become doctors do so from a sincere desire to help others, those who set out to be people leaders should do so because they want to make a positive difference in the lives of the people they serve. That's right, *the people they serve.* That's what an effective leader is doing: serving the people in their team. Throughout this book, we'll explore some of the traits of poor leadership that I have experienced and highlight the impact these have on people. More importantly, we'll see what good leadership looks like and provide some quick tips on creating highly engaged teams. This book is not a high-brow academic text on leadership philosophy, and it's certainly not exhaustive. It is more a down-to-earth, informative read intended to be thought-provoking and encourage a degree of self-reflection. I hope it will create a spark of change in you if you are a people leader yourself or aspire to become one. In short, we'll move away from boss like behaviours to positive people leaders and create an environment where every day is a great day to come to work!

So, can anyone become a leader?

CAN ANYONE BECOME A PEOPLE LEADER?

Sooner or later, we all hear some version of the following:

> "They were promoted to the leadership role
> because they have excellent technical skills. They
> are the best at what they do."

I am sure there are exceptions to what I am about to say—in extremely technical fields like engineering, for example. However, from what I have seen throughout my career, this outdated philosophy, whereby someone great at their specialist job gets tapped on the shoulder to lead the team, is fraught with the risk of failure for the individual and the people they lead. It's awesome that they are great at what they do, so let them be great at that and advance with breadth in their roles. But are they as great at leading people? Do they have people skills? Will they help nurture the talent they are working with, or will they simply be directive/autocratic, knowing (or at least thinking) they can do it better—after all, they're the technical expert!

The CEO of a business I once worked with had several unsavoury personality quirks, chief amongst them a conviction that he was the best at everything and putting others down. He would critique the work of those who worked for him and be damming of the most minor issue that he disagreed with, many of which were simply a matter of subjectivity.

Reality check: Being judgmental of others' work rarely if ever helps them learn. Constant fault picking, particularly in matters of subjectivity has a habit of leaving people frustrated and confused.

I have witnessed first-hand the impacts of the negative influences of such management in another organisation too. The turnover rate of people in this business was so high that in my 30 years of leadership/consulting, I have never seen a business with a people turnover figure of even 10 per cent of what this rate was. Yes, it was that bad! The manager of this business was unfortunately lacking in many of the requisite people leadership qualities; they were a boss not a people leader.

There are differing views on whether great leadership is something we are born with or can be taught. I am somewhere in the middle. Yes, I've got splinters in my backside from sitting on the fence. I do absolutely believe that we can all be taught more appropriate/effective ways of leading—after all, it's why I felt compelled to write this book. If I didn't think you could be helped to become a better leader, I wouldn't be bothering.

Contemporary leadership research documents that emotional intelligence (EQ) is a critical component of successful leaders. No doubt, those with a high EQ were born with a decent quota of it, and I suspect their various life experiences have contributed to its growth through the years. But that doesn't mean that a person born with low EQ can't raise their level.

I'll pause here for a moment of self-reflection. As mentioned in the opening pages of this book, it is a sad indictment on the majority of the leaders I have worked with that few of them inspired me to want to be like them. And I don't mean technically; I mean in a sensory and emotionally intelligent way. I have been told that I have a high EQ (which is just as well because I'm not blessed with a high IQ), and I have the poor leaders of my past to thank, I suspect, for how I have deployed it. I was also horrendously bullied at school, so over the years, I have tuned my style and emotional response based on my memories of how certain negative situations were handled—what language was used, how it was used, what was the impact on me. This, no doubt, contributed to my EQ growth.

In the dark ages of leadership—let's leap back to the 1980s—how many organisations tested candidates for leadership positions on their EQ? Very few, if any. In that same era, how many tested candidates on their IQ? I would suggest most, if not all. I like to

8

think we have come a long way since then, but it's evident that some leaders still place more weight on technical proficiency than EQ. The good news is that EQ can be taught to a certain extent (unlike IQ), in so far as you can compensate for a deficiency.

That said, the simple truth is that not everyone should be a people leader, and not everyone can be a people leader. You know how some people in life should never have children or own pets? Well, the same can be said for leading people.

As leaders, we have a unique opportunity to help shape the lives of those we work with. That sounds deep, but it's true. Picture this. As a leader, you may have a new team member in their very first job. If we nurture the spark in that person's talent, you will have the privilege of laying the foundations that may well become a flourishing career by guiding them through the fundamentals, helping them build their confidence, and allowing them to make mistakes in a supportive environment that encourages them to learn. The confidence they gain will grow and follow them through the rest of their career in the same organisation or elsewhere.

And while I'm at it, it doesn't matter if we seem to be developing the talent for another organisation's eventual gain. If we thought like that, we wouldn't train anybody for fear they might leave us. Consider this: if we nurture, train and develop our team members, they may opt to stay with us and become vital members of our highly engaged team. These engaged and inspired individuals, I suspect, will pay it forward as they progress either breadth wise or vertically through leadership in their careers. Consider this too: if all organisations train their people well, sooner or later you will benefit from an employee, trained elsewhere, who will become a great member of your team.

The flip side, of course, is that we can also shatter someone's confidence through poor leadership. We can be judgemental of mistakes. We can smother them with too much help. We can be overly directive because we just don't get people—that is, we have no EQ. To quote that wise man, Uncle Ben, *With great power comes great responsibility.*[1]

Would you let a lunatic be in charge of an asylum? No? Well then, let's not let people with no EQ lead people—because people with no EQ seriously don't get people!

At this point, I will caution that having a healthy quota of EQ isn't a leader's get-out-of-jail-free card. Yes, it will afford them a good level of gut instinct and potentially even leadership ability. But this responsibility demands some degree of competency too. We all have to sit some form of test to get a driver's licence because of

---

[1] Uncle Ben (uncle of Peter Parker, also known as Spider-Man) made this quote famous, although it dates back centuries to an unknown source.

the risk of serious injury to ourselves or other road users. So, too, it should be with leadership. The opportunity to influence the lives of others should only be given to those who have mastered the fundamentals of leadership—because the risk of causing mental harm to people is considerable. In some fields of work, there's the risk of physical harm to team members, but across the board, the risk of causing/contributing to mental health problems from poor leadership is all too real. I am a big believer in teaching the fundamentals of leadership well before someone has the responsibility—after all, would you throw your kid the keys to your car and say "Enjoy yourself" before teaching the kid how to drive?

So, what are the consequences of poor leadership traits? Well, ultimately, the overarching by-product will be low engagement, which is very likely to result in low productivity and little to no discretionary effort. (Do you really think team members want to give up their own time for a leader who, well, sucks at being a leader or, worse still, is not a decent person?) Everyone's different, of course, and I am sure there are sadists out there who will get a kick out of mucking up people's heads, but if you're trying to build a highly engaged team, I can assure you it's not the way to go!

Let's break this down.

HOW DO YOU KNOW YOU'RE NOT NAILING IT?

TREATING YOUR TEAM LIKE THEY ARE YOUR INFERIORS

In the military and equivalent roles, the need for a chain of command may have its place. But in the corporate world, I don't believe your team need to be constantly reminded that they are lower than you in the hierarchy by referring to them as "subordinates". The word "staff" is almost as bad. You will never hear me referring to my team members, or anyone else's, as either; I simply refer to the team as team members.

Quite a few years ago, a large financial institution I was working for in a General Manager position engaged the services of a US-based consultancy firm to introduce a new sales and customer service methodology. This new approach involved brainstorming on a Monday morning the top things to do that week to improve sales or customer service and then, on a Friday afternoon, sitting with your team to review the outcomes. Now, I wasn't privy to how much this organisation paid for this ground-breaking approach (I suspect it ran well past one hundred thousand dollars). But within two weeks of rolling out the process, I was pleased to hear from my highly engaged team that surely it would make more sense to combine the Monday and Friday meetings into one and save everyone 30 minutes on a Friday afternoon; yes, indeed, it did make sense. That's the difference when you treat your team like a team and not as subordinates. But I digress. You're probably asking why I gave this example here. Well, because the organisation insisted on all managers seeing the instructional videos designed to explain the process. One video, called *How have you motivated your staff today?* was of a live workshop starring the lead consultant from the consulting firm. (Yes, I cringed at the title, too, but there was worse to come.)

So here we have the consultant feasting on the ideas being thrown up from the audience and writing up on butchers paper every little gem uttered. He then turned to a woman who was desperate to enlighten the group on what she had done; the suspense was building as the consultant turned to, let's call her Mary, and said, "Tell us, Mary, just how have you motivated your staff today?" She excitedly recounted her achievement.

> "Well, this morning, when I walked into my office, I went up to my subordinates and said good morning."

This revelation was met with words like:

> "Brilliant, well done, Mary. Acknowledging your
> subordinates will help motivate them."

Spontaneous and overzealous applause ensued from the audience, who were salivating at this fine example of motivational leadership. At this point, I almost saw my breakfast again and thought I had flipped over to a parallel universe—*THIS* was contemporary leadership?

At the risk of being branded recalcitrant, I took my concerns to the Programme Lead and Head of Human Resources. I let them know that I couldn't show that video to my leaders and, from that point on, wanted to review all videos before they were shown in my business division. I explained the contents were at odds with the culture I was building with my team.

Why was this video so disturbing to me? Because:

1) in referring to her team as subordinates, Mary revealed a mindset that saw her team members as inferior;

2) Mary seemed to think her team should feel blessed that she had taken the time from her busy life to wish them

good morning (well, I guess she did think they were inferior to her!).

Sadly, I have frequently worked with managers (I won't call them leaders) who have behaved this way. They would walk in of a morning and march straight to their office, walking past many of their team without even so much as an acknowledgement. When mentoring one such manager on leadership, I pointed out this trait to him. In fairness to him, it was a complete blind spot. This wasn't another "Mary" situation where he thought he was superior to his team; it was more a case of being so focused on the day ahead that he blocked out his team as he walked in. To his credit, when I pointed it out to him, he took the necessary steps to adapt his entrance and even started arriving ten minutes earlier to provide extra time for a quick hello with his team. He also suffered from the affliction of referring to his team as his staff—he was old school. But he soon embraced the new approach of us all being team members. I am pleased to say that, by having an open mind to change and a willingness to adapt, he went on to record one of the single highest increases in team engagement in the organisation.

> Always treat your employees exactly as you want them to treat your best customers.
>
> -Stephen R. Covey

MICROMANAGING

There's a time and a place for close management of your team members; for example, a trainee who is just starting out, a member of your team who is under performance management for underperformance, or for a brief period when a new team member joins your organisation. There may also be certain occupations that require a tight rein on employees, but even within such industries, I would argue that we as leaders can give sufficient rope to the team so that they feel trusted.

While a few people may like the safety net of having someone constantly looking over their shoulder—it spares them from being accountable—it's not the way to build engagement. In fact, it's an engagement killer. Not only does it disempower the team members, but it also keeps the monkey firmly on your back as the micromanager. Worse than this, it makes your competent team members (who should be the vast majority) feel untrusted. Someone who doesn't feel trusted isn't going to perform at their best, and you're never going to see what they're truly capable of if you're constantly checking up on them.

A well-credentialled executive in a business where I once worked suffered from this affliction to an extent that I had never seen before (and hopefully won't again). Let's say a process had steps

A, B, C and D. He would interfere at every step of the way. For example, someone would complete step A, and he would intervene to say, *"Have you completed step B yet? Be sure to complete step B, and this is what you need to do…"*, then do the same in steps C and D. He would critique their performance every step of the way and then complain that the team weren't thinking for themselves. What makes this example truly awful is that he didn't discriminate; he would apply this to every single member of his team regardless of their credentials or experience. I suggested a tailored approach:

> Hey, Mr Executive, why not base your tailored management on the team members' capabilities and results? That way, if someone has demonstrated the required competencies and results, you empower them to act without your intervention.

Positive noises would ensue before he reverted to his usual micromanagement approach. He would not listen when told his team resented it and would continue to complain that they were not "stepping up".

At this point, I'd roll out one of my favourite sayings: *People live up to or down to your expectations.* This is so true. If you, as a leader, constantly think your team members are going to do work of poor quality, then guess what? You will always, and I mean ALWAYS find a way to prove yourself right. Take that executive I was just talking about—he would constantly nit-pick and find holes in people's work because it was impossible to live up to his exacting standards: *You see, they haven't done C yet!* Um, guess what, champ? You didn't give them a chance to! It's fair to say this person was displaying typical narcissistic traits. (Unfortunately, narcissists are often attracted to leadership roles.) If he could have cloned himself, he would have done so because no one could ever live up to how good he was in his own mind.

The reverse is also true and can be just as dangerous. If you blindly think positively of someone in your team, you'll find glimmers of great stuff to support your view, even in the face of some serious shortcomings.

These two approaches are known as the "halo and horn effect". Both are undesirable, but that said, from the results I have seen and generated, being in "Camp Halo" is a far better place to be than "Camp Horn"!

By taking the view at the outset that people, your team, come to work to do a great job, you will find a way to support them with extra coaching, development, and encouragement to help them realise their potential.

Your faith in them does not need to be blind—you can see their shortcomings, but you focus on their strengths. This is a major contributor to engagement.

> Micromanagement is a complete waste of everybody's time. It sucks the life out of employees, fosters anxiety and creates a high-stress work environment. Select the right people and give them room to get on with the job.
>
> *-Brigette Hyacinth, Leadership First*

CRITICISING TEAM MEMBERS IN PUBLIC

In the Western world, public floggings went out of vogue in most countries quite some time ago. So, too, should public shaming. In my opinion, there is no place for public shaming of your team if they happen to mess up. They're human; mistakes happen. Arguably, the act of airing their dirty laundry in public does to them mentally what public floggings would do physically—hurt them deeply, and not only them but the team members who observe the behaviour.

The wider team will feel bad for their shamed colleague (unless they revel in seeing colleagues shamed), and there's a good chance they will also wonder what you will do to them if they happen to mess up. In short, criticism should always be behind closed doors; it's humane and provides the recipient with the opportunity to put forward their view in what should be a safe environment.

Naturally, if there has been a fundamental breakdown in the process, you need to find a way to communicate this to the wider team so that it's not repeated. However, it's usually possible to do it in a way that maintains the anonymity of the perpetrator.

Some of you may well be reading this and thinking to yourself, "Well, what about someone being just terrible to work with and everyone thinks they're getting away with it? That's an engagement killer too." Firstly, well done, that's very astute and will be the next poor trait I'll highlight, but again, there's a humane way to deal with it that will ensure the ongoing engagement of your team.

Just because your team don't see public shaming doesn't mean they won't notice the action you take over this terrible employee's conduct. Trust your coaching ability. Your team should see the by-product of that team member's counselling (or their exit if they don't turn around their performance).

WALKING PAST POOR PERFORMANCE

Oh yes, indeed, this is a sure-fire way to pour water on the flames of engagement. Picture this. You've got team members in your business pulling 9, 10 or longer hour days and, more importantly, generating some stellar results, and they see team members doing the minimum (or less), with at best mediocre results. How long will it be before your hardworking and successful team members lose interest?

While you can mask the issue by rewarding the high-performing team members (which should be a given), this won't by itself resolve the issue. Resentment will still set in. In a highly engaged team, there is no room for passengers anyway, so timely coaching discussions should be a cornerstone of your leadership. By dealing with performance issues quickly, humanely, and constructively, you will reap the reward of having an engaged team. They will see the results of your actions without you having to hold a ritual public flogging.

MEASURING SUCCESS BY HOURS WORKED

As someone who grew up in the 1970s and 1980s, I remember
well the unions battling business leaders over the issue of a 35-
hour week. The desire to work fewer hours for the same salary
was often championed with varying degrees of success. Most
employment contracts I have signed in my career have been for a
37- or 37.5-hour week, and in how many of these roles do you
think I did only the minimum required? That's a resounding zero!

Over the years, some organisations have used clocking-on-and-
clocking-off systems to record hours, paying excess hours in
overtime or time off in lieu. But many employees of the current
era simply donate their extra time (again, this depends on the
industry as I suspect some still cling to the recording of time).
Some business leaders count on this because it helps them keep
the headcount lower. As there's no escaping the fact that an
engaged team will put in extra discretionary effort, this is cool—to
an extent! However, it's a slippery slope when the goodwill of
your people is taken advantage of—that is, if you don't give back.
Go on, surprise your high performers with some extra time off for
their efforts. You'll be amazed at how highly regarded this simple
gesture will be.

What's worse than taking advantage of your high-performing team's goodwill is the draconian expectation that, even though the team is contracted to work 37 hours a week, they must do 60 hours "because that's what happened when I was more junior". Yes, the executive I referred to in **Micromanaging** was a champion in this area too, and I don't mean that in a good way. Despite working eight hours a day himself, he expected even the most junior team members of his business unit to be doing 10- or even 12-hour days. I know he's not the exception here, as I've seen and heard it myself across many organisations.

If you have tendencies in this direction, please do ask yourself what's more important: the hours your team members work (bearing in mind what they are contracted for) or their outputs? Call me new age, but I would vote on the outputs any day of the week. If someone is able to execute their role to a high standard in less than the required hours in their contract, good on them; hours of work shouldn't be a badge of honour! We live in an era of more and more people desiring balanced work and home lives, so if we, as leaders, can help them achieve that, we should. Our reward? Engaged teams!

As with everything, there is no one-size-fits-all approach, and it's wrong to assume. Learn from my mistake here. In a large financial services organisation where I headed up Operations, I made a habit of randomly walking the floors of my building of an evening to say good night to those of my team who were still there when I left, when time permitted. I would pick 2–3 floors each day. There was a woman on my leadership team who was high performing. I had handpicked her and promoted her into the role, and she had quickly sealed her position as my deputy. Across a six-week period, I noticed that no matter what time I would finish up, she was always still there, so I would say something like, *Come on, it's time to go* or *Go home and relax*, or joke, *Haven't you got a home to go to?*, thinking this would show her I had her best interests at heart. One day in our regular one-on-one meeting, she asked me, "Can I please give you some feedback?" to which I replied, "Absolutely". (Feedback should always be seen as a gift because it provides a golden opportunity to adapt.)

She went on to explain that working the hours she did was her choice, that it wasn't a chore or a sign of a problem—she simply loved her job. But she felt wretched when I repeatedly suggested she should leave at the same time as I did. What a revelation! There I was thinking I was doing the right thing when, in fact, I was potentially eroding her exceptional engagement level.

With that feedback on board, I adjusted my behaviour. From then on, I always first sought to understand why people were still there when I left. As GM, it was invaluable for me to be able to differentiate between:

- those who genuinely wanted to be there because they loved their role (music to my ears, as long as they weren't at risk of burnout)

- those who had to be there because of insufficient resources through an incorrect headcount or absenteeism

- those who were poor time managers, Or

- those who just wanted the GM to see them working late!

Appropriate action, or in some cases inaction, could then ensue.

CREATING A CULTURE OF FEAR

I won't spend much time on this poor trait as it should be largely self-explanatory. Put simply, this approach to people management (I won't give it the compliment of calling it leadership) is well and truly past its use-by date. It's draconian and, frankly, has no place in the current work environment (in case you haven't noticed, I'm not a fan!). Sadly, there are still leaders out there who use this as their go-to style. If this is your style, you have purchased the right book, so please be open-minded! Creating a culture of fear may work for a short period—just until your team can find a better place to work.

A CEO I have worked with regrettably had his head stuck in this zone. He wanted an engaged team with low people turnover, but he also wanted them to fear him or leadership in general. *They need to see heads on sticks* was one of the nuggets he would often roll out. I am sure if it had been legal, he would have used a cattle prod!

As I explained to him, a highly engaged team cannot co-exist with a culture of fear; it simply can't. Let's not confuse consequences with fear. Everyone needs to understand boundaries and that breaking them can have consequences, but consequences don't need to be in your face. They are just there acting as guard rails in the background if something goes wrong. By fear, I mean a culture of "If you don't get this extra 20% of work done in an hour less than it would take you to do the normal amount, I'll need to reconsider your employment" kind of thing, a head on a stick kind of draconian thing!

Unapologetically, I call that weak leadership. Any organisation that permits this tactic either doesn't have the right leaders or doesn't have the right teams. This may sound idealistic, but your team should generate results for you and your business because they feel inspired to do so by you as their leader—not because they break out in a cold sweat at the thought of losing their job!

> Corporate culture matters. How management
> chooses to treat its people impacts everything for
> better or for worse.
>
> *-Simon Sinek*

HOLDING FACT-FREE DEBATES

This one is a pet hate of mine, so please indulge me. As leaders, we're there to inspire our team towards grand goals to fulfil the high-level purpose of the organisation we work for (or own). Have you ever encountered a person who is a champion of generalisations? Sadly, they often hold leadership positions. Something goes wrong, and suddenly everything is rubbish— the team, their work, the last five years' effort, it's all just garbage. Yeah, that person. So instead of dealing with this one issue appropriately, everything is generalised—that's a fact-free debate.

If there's an issue or a problem, it's always good to deal with it straightaway—a stitch in time and all that. But it's also a good strategy to deal in facts and not anecdotes or generalisations. Another issue here of the same ilk is jumping on an alleged issue based on hearsay:

> "Jane said the results coming out of your team are
> not where they should be."

OK, great, so what should the results be, and how do the actual results compare to them? This should be obvious. By being specific and using facts, the person you're speaking with has an opportunity to grow.

The same goes for giving positive feedback: "Well done, Jane, you did great work yesterday" may give Jane a momentary buzz of pleasure. But if you want to see her repeat the good work, tell her specifically what she did well:

> "Jane, that work you did on preparing the monthly report was great; I particularly liked the layout and how you presented the results."

This makes what Jane did tangible and repeatable.

SPREADING NEGATIVITY

We encounter all types of people in life; it's a large part of what makes life interesting. But the variety may include toxic people who spread a vibe of negativity. Don't be one of them because such people make for a genuinely unpleasant workplace.

If the people in your team are negative, your role as their leader will be harder. But if you (or your manager) are negative—well, that's a recipe for disaster. In writing this book, I came across the following quote that resonated well with some examples I have seen:

> When a toxic person can no longer control you, they will try to control how others see you. The misinformation will feel unfair, but stay above it, trusting that other people will eventually see the truth, just like you did.
>
> *-Inspirational Quotes Journal*

When leaders behave this way, it can be because they don't know what success looks like, and it's safer for them to create chaos as a distraction. They like to undermine others to make themselves look good. That's why the above quote resonates. I once worked with a business leader who played in this space, pitting team member against team member through the negative spin he placed on them to others. As this quote suggests, others soon see through this behaviour and, as leaders, we most certainly shouldn't operate this way—it's hardly role modelling what success looks like, is it?

The best advice I give to people caught in this situation is to rise above it. Don't get involved in the negative rhetoric. Instead, take what you've heard, raise it constructively and seek to understand; if nothing else, it will demonstrate that you won't tolerate such behaviour. Essentially, a leader is there not only to lead but to serve their team.

The reality is, if that leader doesn't change their ways, good people will leave. A little-spoken-about role of leaders is to manage upwards. Managing upwards sometimes means having tough conversations with your manager. It is confronting, absolutely it is, but it can also be hugely rewarding when a breakthrough happens.

In seeking to understand why this leader is being toxic, you may well be able to help them navigate a pathway out of it. Leaders don't have all the answers; often, they rely on their team. By no means am I sanctioning the toxic behaviour of a leader; quite the opposite. However, if we can isolate the reason, everyone benefits. In short, we shouldn't tolerate this behaviour from our team members, and we shouldn't tolerate it from leaders. Repeatedly addressing the issues as they arise is the only way to make a positive change!

SETTING UNREALISTIC TARGETS THAT ARE IMPOSSIBLE TO ACHIEVE

A few of the traits already covered tend to display this one as a natural by-product (e.g., **Creating a culture of fear** and **Micromanaging**), but it does warrant calling out on its own. Later in this book, I'll cover the positive traits and how these inspire. One of those traits will be setting realistic targets. For now, let's focus on the dark side!

Unless you've been truly blessed, the chances are you've worked for a leader who is impossible to please. For example, your leader asks you to achieve sales of $100,000 in a month; you achieve $110,000 and receive this response: "Why wasn't it $120,000?" or "Clearly, the target was too low." These people are engagement killers; no doubt, you were feeling pretty damn good about yourself until you received that nugget of feedback.

Setting unachievable targets is a cynical means of never having to pay out on incentives (if the business has them) or is used as a tool for those leaders who like to create a culture of fear; either way, it's a shortcut to low engagement. The reality is that, when faced with impossible targets, people usually feel deflated before they begin, so they don't even bother. The analogy I like to use here is this: you go to a restaurant and order something you think you'll enjoy, but when it arrives, the size of the portion is so big you lose your appetite (*or is that just me?*).

In all seriousness, how I explain this to leaders who tend to have this trait in their playbook is to put it like this. The team need to feel what success looks like—to taste victory, as it were. If they are on a constant cycle of "Your sales target for this month is $120,000" against a backdrop of only ever achieving $90,000, it's safe to say they will be lacking the motivation to go for it, especially if there have been no other business changes to contribute to an uplift.

If, on the other hand, you, as the leader, have some analysis done and it demonstrates that the best salesperson in the business achieved $95,000 in each of the preceding six months while yours couldn't get above $90,000, you might feel motivated to set $95,000 as your target with a stretch of $100,000. When you've hit $96,000, you'll feel amazing and try even harder to reach that bit further towards the $100,000.

I experienced this in an organisation where the revenue for the previous few years had shown incremental improvements. Suddenly, at the beginning of the new financial year, the CEO announced he expected the cumulative efforts of everyone to be better than 50% of the entire previous year's turnover and that each team's objective would be a chunk of that. What this meant, in reality, was having to deliver double the highest previous result they had recorded to achieve their incentives. He thought this was completely fine; after all, he was the boss. Needless to say, the team quickly became deflated. After a short period into this new arrangement, he was able to be convinced that, with nothing else changing, the targets were impossible—a dangerous way to start the year with head-hunting recruitment firms constantly trying to lure the team away. The targets were reduced to a more achievable level with some stretch built-in for added incentive. Following the end of the quarter, revenue was a very healthy 50% higher than the corresponding period in the previous year because of the incremental uplift in targets, the engaged team and, yes, some bloody hard work.

Naturally, there are occasions in business when backs are against the wall, and everyone needs to dig deep to deliver an additional 10–20% performance; let's not get confused with those times. I'm talking about the ongoing bread and butter objectives. One of the key traits for building and sustaining engagement is celebrating successes, which we will touch on later. Can you imagine a culture where the targets are set so high that they're rarely or never achieved? It's safe to say there wouldn't be many celebrations around the place!

TRYING TO BE EVERYONE'S FRIEND

The opposite of the leader who creates a culture of fear is the leader who loves to be loved. An area of confusion for many arises when they think engagement is about being loved by your team members. But you don't have to be loved by everyone to build highly engaged teams.

Naturally, it is pleasant to be in a position where you're liked as well as respected as a leader. There's nothing wrong with that. In fact, from my experience, when you are liked, as well as respected, your team will often stretch themselves even further. Let's face it, no one said you had to be horrible to be a leader, did they? But when you confuse engagement with popularity, you are on the road to reaping poor results. Why? Because you'll be so focused on making popular decisions that you'll lose sight of the business imperatives. There is also the risk you'll end up in the camp of the leader who walks past poor performance—you don't want to rock the boat, do you, or make yourself unpopular? Not only will your results go south, so too will your team's respect for you. When there's an element in the team on cruise control that you're ignoring (you don't want them to be upset with you, do you?), your strong-performing team members will rightly feel like they're carrying the weight of everyone. Sound familiar?

From my experience (yes, in my fledgling days of people leadership, I did allow myself to focus on popularity, but a few bad results soon whipped me into shape!), if we focus on a people-first approach—that is, coaching, developing, rewarding, having your team members' backs, and counselling them when things go wrong—the natural by-products are respect, trust, and engagement. Be consistent in that approach, and you shouldn't be hated (although there's no accounting for taste).

This is a building block towards sustained engagement. Importantly, it's not a style you can opt-in and opt-out of when it suits you or the business. It has to be embraced as a constant, or you're not really people first, are you? Let's be clear once again—being people first does not mean trying to win a popularity contest; it's about having the people who look to you for leadership at the forefront of your mind. That is when the magic happens.

> You can please some of the people all of the time,
> you can please all of the people some of the time,
> but you can't please all of the people all of the time.
>
> *-John Lydgate*

UTTERING THESE GEMS

If you catch yourself saying any of these, your leadership credentials might be suspect.

Don't keep a dog and bark yourself

Your team members should know you're their manager/leader. Do you need to remind them of their so-called subordinate status? Reinforcing their alleged inferiority to you as their leader only serves to create a division between you and them. By creating such a division, do you feel that you'll get the most out of them? Will they feel comfortable being open with you? Will they come to you with a problem/issue before it becomes a crisis?

I've got the stripes on my shoulder

Yes, a manager, and quite a senior one, once said that nugget to me—in fact, more than once. This put-down may have its place in the military services, although I suspect contemporary leadership has got a foothold there, too, but certainly not in private enterprise. It's another way of saying 'I'm the boss' which is equally as bad.

We need heads on sticks

This beauty was said repeatedly to me by a senior leader (perhaps a reincarnated warrior of old?) who, at the same time, wanted his team members to be engaged. Let's be clear: a culture of fear cannot coexist with an engaged team because if team members are looking over their shoulders in fear, they're not going to be engaged.

Our number one value is shareholders, then customers, then our team

Great, so, as a team member, you rank third. A contemporary leader should know that, without their team humming, customers won't be happy, and there will be little uplift in shareholder value. So, flip it. Team members come first. You coach, nurture, develop, recognise, counsel when things don't go right and reward when they do. The team will feel engaged, the customers will experience the by-products of that, and they'll then add value to the shareholders by sticking around, purchasing more, and being a referrer.

WHAT WILL POOR PEOPLE LEADERSHIP GIVE YOU?

Here are a few side-effects you may have seen as a result of each of the poor leadership traits we have touched on.

HIGH ABSENTEEISM AND PRESENTEEISM

Let's define these terms first. *Absenteeism* is about being absent from the workplace for unscheduled reasons (i.e., we're not talking about holidays or training days here); presenteeism is about being present in the workplace but unproductive for whatever reason.

A higher-than-usual absenteeism rate (lots of sick leave and stress leave or even absence without leave) is a sure sign your people don't want to come to work. There will be seasonal variations, of course (flu season etc.), but anything higher than 5–6% absenteeism (and I'm being generous here) should ring alarm bells. If your absentee rate regularly exceeds this, it's costing you money—for example, is it making you have to employ extra people? Or are timeframes for projects getting blown out?

Presenteeism is more insidious because it's harder to detect and measure. People who are not engaged may still turn up to work, but they just go through the motions, collecting their pay, smiling at the boss, and contributing very little.

How much more successful can your business be if all of these people function to their full potential? What are the customer service impacts and the impact on your brand?

A LACK OF TRUST

If you're unapproachable or don't listen to your team, will they come to you when an issue arises? I suspect not. This issue could lead to procedural breakdowns, and unless you go digging, the chances of discovery may be remote.

In a business I worked with several years ago, there was a significant breakdown in risk controls. Audit findings and recommendations for improved controls weren't acted on. A member of the team exploited this and was able to commit a fraud that ran into millions of dollars. That was bad enough. But what was worse for me than the financial impact was that this was entirely preventable. Yes, had management acted on the audit's recommendations, the fraud could not have been committed. Colleagues of the person committing the fraud knew something wasn't right, yet the "closed-door" style of leadership of that division meant they didn't speak up. Some were scared of getting their heads ripped off, and others figured, "If management can't be bothered, why should I?" The fraud came to light within a fortnight of installing new leadership with a fresh perspective. *Scary, huh?*

DISAPPOINTING RESULTS

If your team members aren't engaged, will you achieve the best results possible? Sure, you might occasionally hit a goal, but will this be sustainable? From my observations, the answer is a resounding no!

A team that is truly engaged will be self-actualizing.[2] They will want to achieve the results because they *want* to achieve the results, not because they've been told to. An engaged team will put in a large discretionary effort, whereas a disengaged one will do the minimum.

You would be surprised at how the smallest thing can trigger an uplift in engagement and, therefore, results. Early in the COVID-19 pandemic, a business I was consulting with had no capability to work from home; indeed, the head of the business was fundamentally opposed to it as he didn't trust the employees would work. I was able to convince him to trial it and so I developed the capability for them to do so.

---

[2] Self-actualizing is a technical term used to refer to the ability to become the best version of yourself—that is, to reach your potential.

In the lead-up, the team were doing the minimum hours, and this had been a long-standing by-product of low engagement; overlay this with genuine fear amongst the team of the impacts on their health of the virus. Within two days of enabling working from home, there was an uplift, but as the saying goes, *One swallow does not a summer make.* Soon we would see a genuine and sustained uplift in engagement because they felt that management had listened to their concerns and cared. This resulted in a 25% uplift in productivity, and some 12 months later, it had (together with other factors) led to a 70% uplift—without a word of a lie. That's the biggest turnaround I have ever witnessed. No process change, no system enhancements, just an uplift in engagement. This uplift led to an increase in discretionary work hours from each team member. Why is it hard for some leaders to understand that if you take care of your teams, they will take care of you and your customers?

Quite a few years ago, in a large financial institution where I was leading operations, we introduced Six Sigma as a productivity and customer experience improvement methodology. Now, a number of businesses would simply hire consultants for this activity. The consultants would come in, shave off some dud processes, and then leave. We took a different approach. We trained a group of business analysts to do this work. They then proceeded to pick off the low-hanging fruit, and the immediate results were awesome.

This business unit of circa 1,000 people had an overall people-engagement score of 85%, which was close to the world's best practice, as defined by the measurement tool used at the time. Team engagement was so strong that some members sought training in Six Sigma so they could identify deeper process improvements (within due controls, otherwise it would have been a free-for-all). The net result was an annual productivity gain of some 10–12.5% with little or no system enhancements.

In another institution, I led a division that improved to the point where this comparatively small unit that generated 10% of global revenue began generating 21% of global profits. It's no coincidence that it also had the highest people-engagement scores of the group globally, matched with industry-leading Net Promoter scores for customer satisfaction. So, you see, the right leadership leads to high engagement, and the desired results then follow.

HIGH PEOPLE TURNOVER

People leave managers, not businesses. That's a generalisation as I am sure people also do leave businesses they don't like; however, it is more common that people leave their jobs because they think their leader, um … sucks. Yes, that's right. Pay and conditions, no doubt, also feature, but arguably that's also a result of a leader who isn't in tune with their team members.

A pet hate of mine is when people go to resign because they've been offered more money elsewhere, and suddenly the business leader puts their hand in their pocket and offers to match it. Firstly, the understandable reaction to that is, "Why didn't you pay me what I deserve before I had to resign?" Secondly, those who are convinced to stay generally leave a short while down the road because the issues they had with their leader were still there!

I have read that the true cost of people turnover ranges from 50 to 150% of the salary of the people that leave, depending on the nature of the role. This includes recruitment fees, training costs, loss in productivity, and lost opportunity costs.

Therefore, it's fair to say that anything over double-digit turnover is costing your business tonnes of money. A business I was consulting to had a turnover bill estimated to be more than $2 million in the year before I started (hence one of the reasons I was engaged).

Can you afford to have poor leadership in your business?

FIFTEEN TIPS FOR CASTING A POSITIVE LEADERSHIP SHADOW

You may have heard the term "leadership shadow" and wondered what it meant. There are numerous texts available that dig into the science behind the term, but my definition is simple: it's the impact of your leadership style—*what are the people impacts of the things you do or say?* A negative metaphor for this is *When that leader sneezes, the whole team catches a cold*, meaning that if you're having a bad day, your team suffers (well, that's my interpretation anyway!). The same also applies in reverse. If you're a positive, inspiring leader, it stands to reason this will flow on as a positive influence on your team.

As the leader, regardless of your level in an organisation, you set the tone for those who work with you. If you're a generally unpleasant individual who has a reputation for not caring less about your team, this will inevitably create a negative vibe in your culture and all the accompanying cultural traits will follow. However, if you are a positive, caring, inspirational leader (to name a few traits), your culture will have this shadow cast across it, and the results will follow.

Taking a people-centred approach to leadership means ensuring your team members receive the support they need (including training, development and coaching). Reward them when they do well; counsel them sensitively when things don't go well; give them appropriate challenges and "catch them doing the right thing". When team members are happy at work, this happiness flows into excellent service to clients (internal and external), and ultimately it adds to the bottom line. Moreover, it creates a positive perception of your business as an employer of choice. People want to work for successful businesses, and they want to work in businesses where they know they will be treated well. Wouldn't it be a great position to be in to have highly credentialed and talented people queuing up to join your business because it is highly regarded as an *employer of choice?*

We've discussed several negative traits of leadership and their various impacts through the stories I have shared in this book up until now. Now let's flip this around into some tips for casting a positive leadership shadow.

> Take care of your employees and they will take care
> of your business. It's as simple as that.
>
> *Sir Richard Branson*

1: CREATE A SET OF VALUES, LIVE THEM, AND HOLD EVERYONE ACCOUNTABLE TO THEM

If you are part of a large corporation, it probably already has articulated its values; however, you still need to live them and hold everyone accountable to them. If you are part of a small to medium-sized business, or a new business, you may well get the chance to help articulate the values. If you have your own business, you might not have gotten around to this task yet. Should that be the case, I strongly encourage you to identify those values relevant to your organisation's purpose and the culture you want to foster.

The values you create should become the DNA of your business. If done correctly, they will be the compass for everyone on your team when making decisions. Everything will emanate from them; the plans and objectives should be in line with your values, which, in turn, should be in sync with the purpose of your organisation.

It's always good to arrive at a small number of values that are relatable to everyone in the business—I suggest no more than five or six. There are different ways to approach this exercise. One way is to present them as a list of stand-alone words, perhaps with a description or a series of phrases that clearly define the expectation. For example, the following could be used:

> **Integrity**. We always act with integrity and deal honestly and transparently with our colleagues, customers and stakeholders.

Or your value statements could be simple sentences such as:

> **We always act with integrity.**

I have not worked in a business that didn't feature integrity (or similar) as a value. Others should be unique to what you and your team value. Common themes are customers, people, agility, innovation, teamwork, community. There are, no doubt, many more.

Usually, the creation of values is leader-led, but that doesn't mean you can't have a few team members working with you. You could come up with a long list and turn this over for culling by the wider team. Or you could present a blank canvas where you create the values together. Either way, it is a powerful group exercise.

Once you have arrived at your final list of values, it's always a great idea to workshop them with your overall team(s) so that they understand them thoroughly and buy into them. In short, you can't just launch a set of values and expect everyone to flick a switch and start living them straightaway; it will take change management. I find it useful as a leader to paint a verbal picture of what the new environment will *feel like* because you cannot *see* a workplace culture: you *feel* it, and what you value is at the very core of the culture. By describing the environment you want to create, everyone will come to understand what is required of them, a big step towards the changes you desire.

Once you decide the values, you need to communicate them. Display them prominently in your work environment, where they will be a constant reminder to workers. Put them on workstations, in meeting rooms, and even in a reception area for your customers and stakeholders to see. Remember, these values show others what you stand for, and they will help you and your team arrive at day-to-day decisions.

After launching the new values, what next? Well, arguably, it's the next step that is the most important one you'll take—*holding people accountable to them.* OK, yes, creating the values is also important, but that step is pretty pointless if you're not going to call out contrary behaviours or recognise the desirable ones. Later in the book, we'll discuss performance reviews. As I explain there, reviewing performance against the values is critical to building an engaged workplace culture—this sets the tone. It shows that it's not just what you do but how you do it that gets rewarded (or otherwise).

Undoubtedly, anyone acting contrary to the values must receive timely and specific feedback that allows them to correct their course. This is not only important for them but also for their colleagues. In a values-driven environment, there should be nowhere to hide. We should all hold each other accountable: peer to peer, manager to team member and team member to manager, values are the glue that binds us all together. If your team sees no action taken for noncompliance with the values, they'll soon start to see those values as empty, meaningless, and optional; this is when they check out!

As well as calling out behaviours that are contrary to your values, it is always a great idea to celebrate success. (Later on, we discuss communication and celebrating successes.) Sharing examples of excellent work that demonstrates the organisation's values is a fantastic way to inspire others to follow suit. I tend to do this immediately so that it's even more powerful. For example, the customer is generally at the centre of most values, so when a customer compliment comes in, I share this with the team as "an excellent example demonstrated by Mary of our Customer value of …" If a complaint is received, I tend to share those, too, but withhold the name of the person responsible (it's called "public praise, private criticism"—see more about this later).

Finally, I like to create awards based on the organisation's values. It provides the opportunity to create role models for the business who will further enhance the culture. Have some fun with it. You could have novelty trophies that don't cost much money; it's the act of celebrating what these role models have done that is important, not the type of reward.

> The CEO is not in charge of the company. The values are. If, at the end of our careers, we have not passed along positive values, we have abdicated our leadership role.
>
> *-Dave Logan, PhD*

2: ENSURE EVERYONE UNDERSTANDS THE VISION AND THEIR ROLE

> Vision without action is merely a dream. Action
> without vision just passes time. Vision with action
> can change the world.
>
> *-Joel A. Barker*

A mistake easily made is for the leader to have a clear vision of where they want to take the business and be so passionate about it that they charge ahead, look back and find nobody behind them. Why? Because they didn't articulate their vision to the team and get their buy-in, which, unless you're a sole operator, is indispensable.

An organisation's Vision statement doesn't need to be updated frequently and arguably shouldn't be. It should stay in place for at least three years (possibly longer) or until it's close to being achieved. In fact, it should be a significant enough stretch, without being impossible, to be hard to achieve. If you are part of a large corporation, the senior leadership team tends to create the Vision statement; if you are part of a global enterprise, you may have an overarching Global Vision with each country then having a domestic one. Once you have a Vision statement, the strategy for achieving it follows.

Given the relative infrequency that a Vision statement gets updated, it should be straightforward for everyone in the business to understand it. From my experience, this is an assumption not met by reality. If your team members don't understand the Vision statement, how can they support you in achieving it? Taking this to the next level, if a team member doesn't understand the Vision statement, how do they understand the role they play in its achievement?

My job here isn't to teach you how to write a great Vision statement for your business, but here's a few examples of good ones so you get the idea. Note the simplicity.

> Instagram: "Capture and share the world's moments"

> Oxfam: "A just world without poverty"

> TED: "Spread ideas"

> Ben & Jerry's: "Making the best ice cream in the nicest possible way"

A line I like to include when composing team engagement surveys is: *I understand the vision and strategy of my organisation and the role I play in its achievement.* A yes or no response will serve as a great litmus test for how well the Vision statement is understood.

A team with low engagement will tend to score modestly in this area; conversely, a highly engaged team will score high.

We won't delve into vision and strategy building here as that's a whole book or many books on their own. However, it is critical that, whatever the level you operate at in a large, medium, or small organisation (or your own business), you clearly understand your vision and strategy and can articulate them to those in your area of influence. Consider this: everyone, right through to the most junior person in your business, has a role to play in achieving the vision and strategy, so shouldn't they understand what their role is in doing so? If the answer is no, why are they there?

Invest the time with your team members to ensure they understand the upstream and downstream impacts their role has on the vision and strategy. A perfect example is when processing centres for financial services are sent offshore; traditionally, many organisations only train the people doing this work on a small segment of the process, typically the non-complex and highly repetitive work. Many are not made aware of the downstream impact of what they do (nor, for that matter, of what happened before they received the work for actioning). A business I worked in had a large offshoring centre in Asia. Many divisions were encountering a serious problem—much of the work coming back onshore required rework. My division didn't have this problem because we took a different approach. Firstly, we regarded the team in the offshore centre as an extension of our domestic team, which meant they received the same level of communications and due care as local team members. Secondly, as part of their training, they were given high-level awareness, as a minimum, of what happened in the process before they received the work. Most importantly, they were made aware of the impacts on the customers when mistakes were made. This training was incorporated as a critical component in their induction. Furthermore, whenever customer praise was received, we shared it with the team there; equally, when customer complaints were received on processes they had been involved with, they were given the opportunity to learn from their mistakes. The net result of all of this was:

1) people-engagement scores well above those of every other team in this offshore centre because they felt truly part of something, not just an adjunct to it;

2) very low rework onshore compared to other divisions; and

3) an opportunity to contribute as part of the end-to-end process to industry-leading customer Net Promoter Scores for our division.

It's also well worth the investment to ensure position descriptions, individual objectives, and key performance indicators all align with the overarching business purpose and strategy in a top-down approach. In considering the cascade, where does the baton get passed down to another area/role? Are there overlaps? Are there gaps?

Importantly, ensure everyone understands the role they and their peers and managers play in the business. This is a big step towards the overall business operating as a team to achieve the strategy and ultimately the vision.

> Teamwork is the ability to work together toward a
> common vision. The ability to direct individual
> accomplishments toward organisational objectives.
> It is the fuel that allows common people to attain
> uncommon results.
>
> *-Andrew Carnegie*

3: LEAD WITH EMPATHY

As an overarching principle, those who lead with empathy generally achieve greater levels of engagement. I don't intend for this to be a book laden with technicalities, so I won't list a bunch of stats to support the statement; however, I encourage you to Google the concept and see what you get—it's quite compelling.

I will make one reference:

> Empathy is the most important leadership skill according to research.
>
> *-Brower, Forbes, 2021*

This highlights the staggering difference in engagement levels between having an empathetic leader and not viz:

> 76% of people with highly empathic senior leaders report being engaged, compared to only 32% of people with less empathetic leaders.
>
> *-Catalyst*

Let that variance sink in a bit.

Another compelling metric from the same publication:

> When people felt their leaders were more
> empathetic, 86% reported they were able to
> navigate the demands of their work and life,
> successfully juggling their personal, family and work
> obligations. This is compared with 60% of those
> who perceived less empathy.

What does empathy mean, though, in leadership? Well, put simply, it's walking a mile in your team members' shoes. If I were them, how would I want my leader to behave in this set of circumstances? Naturally, exercise care here because everyone is different. You may be laid back or thick-skinned, for example. However, that's the key: *if I were them*. To be truly empathetic, you need to know your team members and how they are likely to react.

As I write this book, most of the world is still in the grip of COVID-19. This unique period has tested leaders' ability to demonstrate empathy and balance the needs of the business with the needs of employees. I have heard of many examples of leaders getting it wrong. An associate told me about one such example in a business where a leader lacked trust and she was a bully. Similar to one of the examples I outlined earlier, this person was opposed to allowing working from home. They had zero empathy for team members who wanted to work from home even though they had genuine fear of catching the virus or, worse, passing it on to a vulnerable relative. The issue became even more problematic due to double standards.

A team member became unwell with severe bronchitis, but she came to work for fear of the repercussions of not going. Sure enough, she soon had to go home and was then unwell the next day and the day after that; needless to say, the leader had a meltdown with passive-aggressive comments in overdrive. The double standards kicked in when a relative of Mrs Executive who also worked in the business, took time off with a minor ailment which was considered completely ok by the executive. Now, this example stretches beyond lack of empathy into hypocrisy, but as you consider these examples, think about the impact on team motivation.

How would an empathetic leader have dealt with the above situation? Well, firstly, I would hope they would be concerned for the welfare of the sick team member who came to work (of course, she wouldn't have come to work in the first place because she wouldn't have lived in fear of the repercussions of not doing so, but she did, so let's run with it). They would also be concerned about the colleagues of the team member potentially catching it, and well, in these COVID-19-impacted times, that should have heightened the concerns. So, in short, an empathetic leader would have checked in on the team member, asked her how she was feeling, and respectfully suggested she should go and rest up (potentially with a stop off at the doctor's or a COVID-19 testing station on her way home). At the same time, they would have seen if another team member could help out with her workload during her absence, so she wasn't burdened with worrying about that. This, of course, has a twofold positive impact: the team member would know she was genuinely cared for in the business, and other team members would see it as an example of care for their colleague and, frankly, for them. This, in turn, manifests in higher levels of engagement. In the same set of circumstances as described previously, the team also wouldn't resent Mrs Executive's relative for taking a couple of days off to tend to their own minor ailment.

> Being a leader is more than just wanting to lead.
> Leaders have empathy for others and a keen ability
> to find the best in people ... not the worst ... by truly
> caring for others.
>
> *-Henry Gruland*

It's natural and necessary for leaders to be concerned about the business results, and the various lockdowns of the COVID-19 era have certainly tested the stress levels of many. At the risk of oversimplifying things, a people-first leadership style, which has empathy at its core, will make the team want to do everything they can to support the business that supports them. For example, when working from home was first rolled out in a business I was working with, we saw every team member working during much of the period they usually would have spent commuting, because they appreciated being allowed work from home and wanted to give back. Regrettably, the CEO of that business couldn't help himself and then went on to compel people to always donate their travel time if they wanted to work from home; why, you ask, when everyone was already doing it voluntarily? Good question and a perfect example of how team engagement that has increased through empathetic leadership can quickly be undermined. Something I believe goes hand in hand with leading with empathy is not being afraid to demonstrate an air of vulnerability to your team. It demonstrates authenticity and further "humanises" you to your team. Take the whole sorry COVID-19 situation again for a moment. It's OK for leaders to share their fears with their team about the hammering business took and to convey any personal fears about the virus, not to spread panic but in the spirit of "we're in this together".

Ask yourself which leadership style a team would respect more: the leader who says:

"Yes, there's a virus out there. The news reports are exaggerating it. We have work to be done or our business is going to go backwards."

or the leader who says:

"This virus is a concern to us all. There's no escaping the news coverage and, like you, I am genuinely concerned about the impact on my loved ones, myself and you all. No doubt there is going to be an impact on our business, but by us all working together and looking out for each other, we'll get through it."

I suspect option two will garner more support; it shows vulnerability, empathy, and a bit of rallying of the team. Now, of course, everyone's different. Some people prefer the blunt messaging; however, I'd wager most fall into camp two and want a leader they can relate to and can relate to them.

At some time, most leaders are confronted with the unpleasant task of communicating to a team that there's going to be downsizing. Unless you're a sadist, you are not going to enjoy this experience. Once again, a leader who has developed a track record of empathy credits in the team bank by routinely displaying authentic vulnerability should see their team come through this unpleasant event with engagement levels, while dented, still strong. I will discuss the merits of full transparency in more detail later, but this is an area where this approach to leadership plays a significant part in ensuring your team's trust in you doesn't falter. It's OK to tell your team how you feel (without white-anting your business, of course) and that you know how they must be feeling; again, use empathy, walk a mile in their shoes. What do they want to be hearing right now—their leader being cold and saying, "Guys, we're going to be making 10 of you redundant" or you taking them on a journey as to why it's necessary and showing them genuine compassion? I think most people will opt for compassion and understanding. Indeed, I can't think of any examples where empathy is out of place. In my humble opinion, it should be a default position like a reflex.

An empathetic leader doesn't jump on a below-par level of performance from a team member who usually performs to a high standard without seeking to understand what has triggered the downturn. Without prying into the team member's personal affairs, it's fine to ask if everything is OK, offer your support etc. and let them know you're there for them while also pointing out in a humane way that you've noticed their results aren't where they have been. Arguably, in a Utopian work environment, your team member may well have come to you first without you even having to ask because they know you care.

This may all sound warm and fuzzy, and that may not be your natural style of leadership; in fact, you might be reaching for the bucket at the very prospect. However, you can show you care without being warm and fuzzy—at the very least, by not jumping down the throat of your team member for not hitting targets for the first time since forever.

When your business goes through significant change, you will understand, if an empathetic leader, at what point your team is on their own change journey, bearing in mind that not everyone responds to change in the same way. We each adapt at different speeds. Some love change—it invigorates them—while others fear it and start to worry about what's next. Again, a leader with a track record of transparency, as referred to earlier, will reap the rewards of that approach when steering their team through change. If your team members know that you're always open and honest with them, they won't have to fear a nasty surprise lurking around the corner. When change does come along, it will be expected and seamless. Better still, they will even own the outcome. An empathetic leader will have understood where their team is with the change because they take the time to care. It's a two-way street. Because your team know you care about them, they'll care about you and want you to succeed. They'll flag issues with you early on because your mutual success is as important to them as it is to you.

Of course, despite your transparency and empathetic approach, things won't always go smoothly and how you react when the going gets tough is another key aspect to leading well.

4: BE PREDICTABLE

That sounds really boring, doesn't it? Others prefer to call this "being reliable". In the work context, it is one of the most important attributes of excellent leadership. Imagine this scenario: your team member comes to you with a problem today (and ideally a solution because you've coached them so well!). The circumstances in the context of your business are the same as they were yesterday. Is it acceptable for you to behave differently from how you did yesterday when another team member presented you with the same issue? While there may be some random exceptions, the answer is a resounding no.

To some of you reading this, it may seem obvious. But you would be surprised just how many leaders I have encountered over the years whose reaction to the same set of circumstances changed as dramatically as the wind changes direction. Maybe I have just been unlucky with the leaders I have worked for and with, but I can tell you one thing: this trait is an engagement killer. Often these leaders share the trait of moodiness, so the team don't even want to go near them. They fear what their reaction will be. If your team won't approach you with issues, it's a recipe for disaster because it could mean that the innocent and benign matter they wanted to tell you about goes underground and magnifies to the point where it becomes a crisis. It's also symbolic, because if you react badly to something relatively simple and straightforward, how on earth will you react if something major comes along? So that better go underground for sure. "There's no way I can approach you with this issue" is what your team will, no doubt, be thinking.

Remember the lack of trust we touched on earlier when considering the side effects of poor leadership? Well, this fits here too. That fraud was ultimately committed because issues that were obvious to the team went underground. It was easier than speaking up.

It's relatively easy to be predictable when things are going well (at least in theory), but when the going gets tough, when the heat is on, how do you react? Do you wear your moods on your sleeve? We've all had THAT manager where they came into the office with steam coming out of their ears, and it goes downhill from there. Yesterday he was told of the loss of an account worth $10,000, and he took it reasonably well. How's that going to go down today when someone tells him of the loss of an account worth $8,000? My money is on him going postal and, worse still, not even being told!

Large organisations (and, no doubt, smaller ones too) conduct audits every year with a combination of internal and external auditors undertaking this work. One of the key attributes of a quality audit outcome is management awareness of the issues before the auditor finds them (together with solid action plans to overcome them). I have never received an unsatisfactory audit outcome. Why? Because the team members were open with issues up the line without fear of reprisals (note: that doesn't mean serious breaches were not met with consequences when detected). Compare this with divisions I worked alongside where poor audit outcomes were commonplace. These leaders were not approachable, so issues didn't get raised with them, leading to little to no management awareness of the issues. Needless to say, it wasn't just the audit outcomes that were poor; there was high people turnover, high absenteeism, poor customer satisfaction, and below-par financial results. Of course, these issues went beyond predictability or lack thereof, but this was a significant ingredient in a recipe for failure.

I strongly suggest that, as people leaders, we find a way to leave our baggage at the door, wherever it came from. Now I know this seems to contradict the message around being authentic and transparent. Remember, though, predictability is about reacting the same way today as you did yesterday in the same circumstances. If the environmental factors that led to you making a decision yesterday have changed today, then naturally, it's acceptable to give a different response, provided you do so with an explanation so the team member seeking your input doesn't walk away scratching their head.

Taking your bad day out on your team can have the collateral damage of causing erratic business solutions. Just as it's uncool to take your bad workday out on your loved ones at home, the same applies to your work colleagues—although your loved ones will probably tell you you're being an ass, and I suspect your team at work won't. Sure, we all have our moments because we're human. I am talking about being a serial moody person whose team walk on eggshells and won't approach you. If something prevents you from making the judgement call you would usually make, don't be afraid to park it until you're in the right headspace. If time pressures prevent you from doing that, tap into your EQ and place yourself in your team's shoes—it's not opt-in when everything is peachy leadership style. Being predictable is just that: react the same today as you did yesterday and will do tomorrow.

With all that said, we are all capable of having bad days. You may think you're hiding it well, but your team may be more astute than you give them credit for. If you are someone who generally leads with empathy and has a highly engaged team, there's a strong chance they'll notice something isn't quite right by your body language and want to help. That's another by-product of having an engaged team: they will give a damn about you too!

5: SET REALISTIC GOALS

As outlined when discussing the vision and strategy of a business, each team member must have clearly defined objectives and Key Performance Indicators (KPIs). The well-known SMART acronym—Specific, Measurable, Achievable, Realistic and Timely—is the best guide I've seen to writing worthwhile objectives and KPIs.

Let's shine a spotlight on "Achievable". Earlier in the book, in the section **How do you know you're not nailing it?** I discussed how demoralising it is for a team to be set unrealistic targets and the impact this ultimately has on their engagement. At its worst, it can be soul-destroying. I suspect very few people get their jollies from being told or feeling like they're underperforming. Let's flip it around.

I am all for stretch targets emanating from the overall business plan, as these are what help us drive a business forward. Once a team is truly engaged—and I mean they truly embrace the business and work in it as if it were their own (well as close as possible to that degree of passion)—they will lean towards self-actualization and naturally want to do better tomorrow than they did yesterday or today. In my earlier example of the financial institution where I led a large operational area, I highlighted the 10–12.5% annual productivity gain achieved through self-actualizing team members who embraced the Six Sigma methodology. This is a good example of it. I have also seen examples of natural productivity gain through an engaged team just working smarter and, in some cases, harder; occasionally, this was also a by-product of team members working longer hours, not because they had to but because they wanted to.

> A goal properly set is halfway reached.
>
> *-Zig Ziglar*

Back to the goal-setting. *How do you know when a goal or objective you want to set is realistic or a bridge too far?* A good starting point is to look at the average achievements for a similar operational (or sales or whatever your business is) goal in the past. For example, if in the past the average maximum number of "widgets" processed by an individual was, say, 1,000 per month, setting a target of 2,000 widgets to be processed for the month ahead is unlikely to be achievable. Another way of looking at it is to take your highest performers of the previous 12 months and look at what they achieved. Hopefully, through your one-on-one catch-ups, you understand how they achieved it—if not, now's a good time to ask!

Similarly, look at your lowest-performing team members and see how many widgets they could get through, and once again, the same story: you should seek to understand why. You can then start to form a view of what might be achievable. A one-size-fits-all approach may not be appropriate either. If your highest performer is achieving 1,250 widgets per month and your lowest performer, with the same experience level, only 750, it's not fair to stretch your high performer by 10% and your lowest performer the same. Instead, you might suggest that the high performer maintains their excellent productivity while stretching the mid-point by 10% and the lower end by 15%. But it is critical to ensure that the tools are there—and by tools, I also mean competency. You can't expect the lower performers to rise by 15% just by asking them to do it. Do they feel comfortable with their training? Is their personal computer (PC) as fast as that of the higher performer? (*Side note*: I once came across this in a high-volume processing area where the productivity of one administrator was considerably down on the productivity of everyone else. One day, this administrator happened to use another team member's PC and was blown away by its speed. The guy didn't know what he didn't know, so a simple check of such things can make a huge difference.)

As with everything in life, balance is required. Setting goals should never be a case of set and forget. Stay close to the results being achieved and how the team are going. If needed, don't be afraid to adjust up or down incrementally, based on achievement and after consultation. However, don't be THAT person who waits until near the end of the performance period to suddenly move the goalposts when everyone is achieving great results—just to test them. It rarely, if ever, works and one thing you will be successful at is killing morale!

Another approach is to layer your objectives, so everyone will know where they stand come performance discussion time. This means setting a target for each KPI that would "meet expectations". Using the examples highlighted earlier, we might decide that 1,000 widgets per month would meet expectations. Then we would have a layer of stretch targets—in this example, let's say 1,250 widgets per month. Achievement of this target would "exceed expectations". We then repeat this for each of the key objectives.

If you want to make this tool even more robust and transparent, I suggest attaching weightings. These weightings will emphasise those objectives of more strategic and tactical importance. Taking a simple approach, let's be unrealistic and assume there are only two objectives: processing widgets and customer satisfaction. As a business places greater emphasis on customer satisfaction than anything else, customer satisfaction would receive the higher weighting. Let's say a Customer Satisfaction Net Promoter Score rating of 50% is meeting expectations, and one of greater than

60% is exceeding expectations. Given the importance of customer satisfaction, we give it a weighting of 60% compared with widget production of 40%. At the end of the year, the team member has averaged 1,000 widgets per month, which met expectations (weighting 40%), and their Customer Satisfaction Net Promoter Score average across the year is 65%, which has exceeded expectations (weighting 60%). Therefore, that individual has exceeded expectations overall. The benefit of this approach is that it's a transparent way of articulating what "great" looks like. Come performance review time, it creates an opportunity for a much more objective discussion around whether your team member has met expectations or exceeded them.

The above approach to goal-setting is pretty straightforward if you have long-standing processes. But what if you've created a whole new service offering or a new method of measuring team performance? What I have done in the past is create developmental KPIs, which are developmental because they haven't yet been tested. The developmental period could be for just one measurement period of a quarter/six months or, if volatile, it could extend for the whole year. The purpose of the developmental grace period was to ensure the objective was fair and measurable. When I used these, I referred to them as "below the line", so they didn't get counted come performance discussion time if the results were below par. However, when the results were outstanding, they could be considered as part of the overall picture of a team member's work output and attitude.

> A goal should scare you a little and excite you a lot.
>
> *-Joe Vitale*

In most instances, the goals set for an individual in the team should be a subset of the team objectives, which, in turn, should be a subset of the business objectives. This won't always be the case—for example, in a large organisation, the processing of widgets at the micro (team-member) level won't be expressed at the macro (whole-of-business) level. It will probably be bundled into an efficiency ratio or customer satisfaction metric. For all the reasons outlined in relation to the setting of individual targets and their need to be realistic, the same, of course, must be said for setting targets at a team, division, and overall business level.

Often a team member's performance is measured against a combination of individual, team, and business metrics. There is, therefore, little point in being realistic with individual targets only to mess it all up at the team and business level, as these can become equally soul-destroying to the point where team members simply give up. Naturally, the larger an organisation, the more challenging it is for junior or middle-level leaders to influence the overall goal-setting for the business; however, it is still possible to have your say. In every business where I have been Chief Executive, General Manager or Chief Operations Officer, or a level underneath, I have encouraged everyone to submit their feedback on critical components of the business. Otherwise, I would be an ostrich with my head buried in the sand, oblivious to how the team felt about the goals for the period ahead.

Consider this scenario. You, as team leader, believe in your gut that your business can double its revenue in the next 12 months or so. You create a business objective of a 100% increase in revenue and then cascade that to each business unit. Each sub-team of the business unit has metrics with stretches in them. They look at the overall business objective, and their view is that unless there's a material change not accounted for, it's just not achievable. So they'll do one of two things: they'll raise their concerns with you, or they won't.

Hopefully, if you've created the right environment, they'll raise their concerns, and you will have the sense to listen and make the necessary adjustments.

Now, I'll be honest—I have an avid dislike of negativity, so if someone came to me and complained that a 100% increase in revenue wasn't achievable without a solution/compromise suggestion, it would push my buttons. But I would always create an environment where such lofty targets could be discussed openly. Through such discussions, the 100% increase in revenue may ultimately stay but with a clearly outlined proposed enabler to that increase also baked into the business plan. Should that not be executed for any reason, an alternative revenue target would be substituted. *In short, we have to keep it real at all levels of the objective-setting process.*

We'll discuss communication in depth later in the book, but it's well worth touching on now. As I mentioned earlier, establishing goals is not set and forget. It is critical you continually communicate how the team is going against the overall targets. This means complete transparency. You might like to come up with an overall score for the most important business metrics rolled up to a team or business unit or the business as a whole, with a traffic-light system to highlight how each layer is performing. Again, elsewhere we will discuss performance reviews (which are also a must) but, by publicly discussing results (the good, the bad and yes, the ugly), everyone in the team can understand how their results compare to the overall results. If you want to go one step further, you could illustrate the average of each team member's performance against the objectives. This further cements their understanding of their performance relative to the average of their peers and the value they bring to the business, but more on that later.

As with pretty much every tip I'm covering in this book, it's all about:

- dealing with your team members with integrity (always)

- communicating openly (always)

- being open to feedback from the team (always).

Naturally, this doesn't mean always compromising on what you want to achieve for the sake of team harmony, as it's fair to say that doing so will also compromise business outcomes. Sometimes we must be unwavering in what we require while bearing in mind that just because a business objective is critical, it doesn't mean it's achievable under the status quo. Listening to your team will create opportunities to identify problems early and incorporate their thinking into the plan. The earlier we hold these discussions and the more transparent we are with the team, the greater our chance of success.

6: DON'T REPROACH—COACH

I have found the optimum way to continue to build capability and engagement is to adopt a coaching mindset. Encourage your team and seek to have them do better today than yesterday. A highly engaged team will generally respond well to this and seek to improve themselves; however, you still have a role to play in this space, of course.

Consider this scenario. You've set realistic targets, yet you have team members who aren't achieving them. They're well below the standard set by the majority; to your mind, they're holding back the team. How do you bring them up to the required standard while also ensuring you don't lose the motivation of the others? As we've discussed previously, the way **not** to do it is to criticise the under-performers in public. Sure, this will ensure the rest of the team know you're aware, but not only will you probably embarrass the under-performers you will also run the high risk of alienating anyone with any semblance of EQ. They'll be well aware that one day, should their performance fall below par, the same public shaming could be heading their way. The net result is highly likely to be reduced engagement.

From my experience, the performance of an individual doesn't suddenly fall off a cliff. At least not without a sudden trigger inside work or outside. The person is probably new to the role/task and still coming to grips with it, or they've been doing the role for a while, and something is holding them back. It could be complacency and boredom (they've been doing it for too long), poor initial training, system problems, ongoing personal problems, poor organisational skills, or, worse, laziness.

Whatever the reason for the lower-than-required performance, everyone deserves an opportunity to correct their course, and the best starting point is to seek to understand what's going on. Sit down with the under-performer and explain the variance in performance relative to their peers. Ask them—not in an accusatory tone like *"What on earth are you doing?"* (that's not a winning approach!)—but in a coaching style:

> "Joe, I see for the last month you processed 500 widgets, whereas most people in the team processed 750 widgets or above. May I ask, what's in your way?"

Some people will open up straightaway. Others will require some coaxing, but again, your role here is not to make them feel bad but to understand the obstacles.

"Joe, are you having system issues?"

"Joe, are you comfortable that you understand how to process the widgets in the most efficient way? For example, how long does it take you to process one?"

"Are there any disruptions impacting your productivity that I'm not aware of?"

Naturally, you'll adapt your approach depending on where these answers take you, and this list isn't exhaustive by any means.

Once you have clarity, it's time to set an improvement path. If it's a training issue, a great place to start is to buddy this person up with one of your highest performers. This method has two benefits:

1) They'll learn best practice.

2) The higher performers will know, discreetly, that you're across the performance gap and doing something constructive about it.

Sometimes this action alone is enough to kick-start someone's improvement journey, and soon the team member is able to increase their output considerably. As mentioned before, another quick fix could be identifying a system issue with their PC—stranger things have happened!

> If you focus on results, you will never change. If you focus on change, you will get the results.
>
> *-Jack Dixon*

Possibly the most stubborn obstacle to overcome is someone's inherent laziness. If your discussions and observations point in this direction, then a performance improvement plan will be required (and to an extent, you could implement the same if it's a training issue). It will enable you to set clear, incremental targets that you can tightly monitor. Using our widget example, you should set realistic milestones for the individual to achieve by a set date. In the example above, work out what is required every week to reach the minimum 750 widgets per month and set the bar slightly lower, bearing in mind the gap they have to make up—for example, 187.5 are required per week, but they're coming from a position of only doing 125 per week.

Your planned uplift might, therefore, look like this:

1. Week one, achieve a target of 135 widgets—at the end of
    the week what was achieved?

2. Week two, achieve a target of 150 widgets—at the end of
    the week what was achieved?

3. Week three, achieve a target of 165 widgets—at the end
    of the week what was achieved?

4. Week four, achieve a target of 187.5 widgets—at the end
    of the week what was achieved?

The question posed at the end of each target period is a simple yet
critical one. If the team member only achieved 130, you might
want to adjust the next target down. Remember, you want them
to feel like they can do this, that it's not impossible. Equally, if they
bolt out of the blocks and hit 150 in week one, you should
consider raising the next target. In fact, to this end, there's no
harm in setting the target weekly—that is, don't set the entire
improvement pathway upfront.

Assuming this is a dream scenario and your team member is back
on track after an initial coaching exercise, don't consider that as
job done. No, importantly, you should continue to stay in touch
with them, provide positive reinforcements of their achievements

compared to where they used to be, and celebrate the success. A frame of mind to establish here is to check in, not check up!

If, however, the team member isn't responding to the improvement pathway and progress isn't being made, you may need to repeat the first step to understand why. The under-performer must be given every opportunity to improve for their sake, the team's, and the sake of the business as a whole. In the worst-case scenario where you have to exit the team member, you will have documented evidence that you worked hard to turn around their performance.

My preferred approach is to coach up. Regrettably, however, some don't make it and need to be coached out. I won't touch on the exit process as that will vary depending on your jurisdiction. It's not something to be feared as long as you have acted with integrity and taken clear steps to help the individual improve. *If they don't know what's wrong, they can't fix it. Right?*

7: COMMUNICATE, COMMUNICATE, COMMUNICATE!

> The art of communication is the language of
> leadership.
>
> *-James Humes*

Finding the right balance in the frequency of communication is good, but if in doubt, over-communicate rather than under-communicate! We have spoken previously about ensuring everyone understands their role in achieving the strategy—that should be the higher intent of all ongoing communications. Against the backdrop of this strategy, you need to assess how your team members are performing, with particular emphasis on their specific sphere of influence within the bigger picture.

As I have touched on a few times now, open and transparent communication is a must. Not only will it garner you the respect of your team, but it will also yield a very positive impact on your team culture.

> Your ability to communicate with others will
> account for fully 85% of your success in your
> business and in your life.
>
> *-Brian Tracy*

Now, before you jump to the conclusion that this means you have a licence to blurt out any piece of news—good, bad or ugly—that you deem relevant to your team, stop right there.

It stands to reason that you must also consider the other aspects I have spoken about, with particular emphasis on leading with empathy and being predictable—within reason. By "within reason", I mean if you have a habit of delivering good news (which you should), do that consistently. For example, if you routinely share positive news, such as tenders won, record sales, or high profitability, don't suddenly stop doing so without explanation because the team will start to wonder what's going on (it's natural to do so!). Equally, if you share bad news should this arise, you need to do that just as consistently; your team will invariably respect you for not just sharing the good stuff but being honest with them about what's not going so well, and they won't start to second-guess and make up their own version of reality!

The same goes for "the ugly", which I define as worrying news.

It might not happen, but then again it might. A team kept well informed about the business will truly feel a part of it and should have the strength to cope with the uncertain and the unpalatable. If you shy away from sharing such news, are you truly being transparent? Again, the key here is consistency. Your team will come to rely upon your open and honest approach, and if they know that you always deliver all the news you can, they will respect you for it. The emphasis is on *all the news you can*.

Business life, of course, isn't always textbook. There will be times when you are aware of some news that may not go down so well; in fact, it will likely go down like a lead balloon. But you can't share it because it's highly confidential. What do you do then? This is a conundrum because you have promised your team that you will always be open and honest with them, and you're not right now.

The key here is to be open and honest about *that*.
When you set the expectation upfront as the leader about your communication style, be transparent about what that looks like and set an agreement of sorts. For example:

> "As the leader of this business, you have my commitment to communicate with you openly and honestly; I'll share the good news and the not so good. At times this may mean having to share some bad news, and with your permission, I won't shy away from that. However, regrettably, there will be times when I will be bound by confidentiality and won't be free to share something. When that happens, you have my commitment that as soon as I am able to do so, I will."

Should the time come when you can share the ugly news, refer to the above agreement as a way of introducing the news. You could say something like:

> "You will recall I committed to always being transparent with you and sharing all the news I could, whether it be good news or the not so good. I also stated that there would be times when I would be bound by confidentiality and unable to share an item of news, but that I would do so as quickly as I could. I would like to advise you of one such example today.

> "As a result of a downturn in sales, regrettably, it seems likely we will need to reduce the size of our sales team. I will know for certain within the next four weeks, but I wanted to share this news with you now so you might start to consider what the impacts might be for yourself and look at other opportunities within the business"

Now, that's an example of one of the most traumatic messages you will ever deliver as a business leader. Some of you reading this might be thinking I am crazy for suggesting you be transparent about something that may never happen. After all, you might cause unrest. Frankly, there's probably no right or wrong answer.

Yes, you're quite right, the downsizing might never happen (by way of a footnote, I would suggest only sharing such news if you are more than 80% certain it's likely), and you could well trigger resignations or generally cause unrest. Remember, though, it is just one piece of your leadership shadow. If you haven't built the other building blocks that have created trust, you would be unlikely to deploy this approach. Consider this as a counter to the fear you might be creating. What if one of your team members is on the cusp of committing to a large mortgage, a new car, or a holiday that they couldn't afford if they lost their job? You wouldn't want to be the cause of them putting their life on hold for something that may not happen (remember the 80% rule); however, you might be a catalyst for them prudently delaying that decision until they know for sure that all is well. I've been there, and I have been thanked for it.

While I don't want to dwell on this bleak scenario, if you are going to communicate a likely downsizing, you must have the appropriate support infrastructure in place to help those who might be affected. (It stands to reason, by the way, that you will make sure you follow the required protocols of your organisation with this stuff.)

Of extreme importance here is the need to follow through on your commitments for updates. In the example above, you stated that you would know for certain in four weeks, so be sure to re-communicate where things are by that timeframe at the latest; ideally, re-communicate ahead of it. This means under-promise and over-deliver. If you think it's going to be four weeks at the earliest before you can let them know with any degree of certainty, then tell your team it will be five weeks. Delays always occur, and it tends to be on the cusp of finding out when emotions start to run much higher, and even the most engaged team members start to lose focus. Should the final news be the worst-case scenario, then this will, of course, mean you will need to ramp up the support not only for the affected team members but also those who are not directly affected. Invariably those who are not directly affected tend to fear the same could happen to them as you've dented the security they felt with their organisation. I won't go through the steps required in dealing with redundancies as that will vary depending upon your jurisdiction, and it's not the purpose of this example. I wanted to illustrate that, for the best results from your team in building trust, I believe in the all-in approach.

As for the communication mediums, these are many and varied, especially in these COVID-19-impacted times. I encourage leaders to ask the team what they prefer. After all, they're the ones receiving it. If they went to a restaurant wanting steak, you wouldn't serve them tofu. The size of your organisation and your level within it will also have a bearing. The larger organisations tend to have quite prescriptive approaches, which junior leaders need to follow. If you happen to be at this level, it doesn't mean you can't operate within that framework and be creative with your team, but the more senior you are, the more licence you will have to be flexible.

As a rule of thumb, bad news should never be delivered by email. The best-crafted written communication can be misinterpreted, and there's no immediate ability for the team to ask clarifying questions or indeed for you as the communicator to check for understanding. My strong preference is for such news to be delivered in communication forums of an appropriate size. In the example of downsizing above, sometimes this is better done in a way that separates those materially affected from those to whom it's for information only, while, of course, bringing the latter up to speed also. Such forums are best presented in a group setting intimate enough for the audience to ask questions. The use of tools such as Zoom or other video-conferencing software has made this easier during COVID-19 and for those who have business units geographically dispersed.

I encourage good news to be shared in the same way, ideally in a regular communication forum—or "town hall", as some call them. These forums are a great way to stay connected with the larger team. They also ensure that everyone receives the same message at the same time and has the opportunity to ask questions about anything that is unclear. You can also bring in some light-hearted content to liven things up—not everyone is a confident public speaker, so having some light content in there can act as an icebreaker for you and the team.

After delivering the in-person communication forum, it's good practice to support this with written communications. It solidifies the key messages and guards against misunderstandings. You might like to supplement the in-person forums with regular newsletters with timely information for the team. Some organisations use blogs as well. I am not a fan of blogs myself, as I am yet to see one done in a way that is not self-indulgent. Speaking of leadership shadows, they can cause negative perceptions. By way of example, a global organisation I once worked for issued a mandate that air travel was to be kept to a minimum as they were conscious of their carbon footprint and the need to cut costs. Yet the Global CEO's weekly blog read like a travel journal: "Today I write to you from New York where I had the pleasure of ...", or "This week I was in London and took the opportunity to attend an Ashes cricket match". *Needless to say, these blogs didn't go down well!*

Find the right communication mediums for you and your business or part of the wider business. Use the appropriate blend of in-person and written formats. Remember, consistency is the key: don't blow hot and cold. Finally, don't be afraid to survey your team to check on how they're feeling about your communications, and don't be afraid to adapt.

Too often, leaders feel like they must have all the answers, or worse, believe they do. Their way or no way. Well, as they say, pride often goes before a fall.

Many years ago, in a financial institution where I was a General Manager, I was asked to take on an underperforming division and merge it with mine. This particular division had not met service levels overall for close to seven years; its costs were blowing out at a macro-budget level but also on individual unit costs. Every night there would be a fleet of taxis waiting outside the building and stretching down the road adjacent to the office as far as the eye could see. They were there for the hordes of employees exiting from the building as they clocked off at 8 pm from their overtime: overtime that was fruitless. They were like hamsters trying to get away while running on their wheel. To reach profitability, the business unit had to cut costs to the tune of $9 million, and the current head of that business unit had just been shown the door (the third to meet their demise over that seven-year period).

You can imagine how ecstatic I was to be asked to take it on—*how uplifting!* But I have a saying: *every challenge is an opportunity.* This was a great, career-defining one!

A global consulting firm had been engaged to review the operations and come up with recommendations to cut costs and improve service. Needless to say, the expense of using the global consulting firm was enormous. Their plan had already been created, and their invoice ran into the tens of thousands of dollars. At the risk of being impolite, it was rubbish. At its centre was cost reduction (a required outcome), and there were some suggestions to improve service, but the plan largely consisted of motherhood statements, Band-Aids and paperclips.

The centrepiece was to rip the guts out of the business unit and retrench something like 80 people. So, having reviewed this masterpiece of economics, I duly asked the Senior Executive of the Division if I could ignore it. He said, "Sure, do it your way but just remember what happened to the three previous General Managers" (tip, that was a backhanded, not-so-hidden piece of passive aggression if ever I'd heard one!).

I took a few days to reflect on things. I recalled often seeing team members from this division enter the building while I waited for my breakfast at the coffee shop of a morning. My impression was that they dragged their feet, were sullen, uninspired, and generally there against their will. I checked their people-engagement score and had my observations confirmed. At 35%, it was one of the worst I'd seen, particularly when compared with the rest of my business unit, which enjoyed engagement overall of 85% with pockets above 90%. Before anything else, I needed answers as to why it was so low, so I did the unthinkable, according to my predecessors, and asked them.

I walked the floors, called meetings, sat on desks, all to garner the unfiltered views of as many of them as I could. A common theme soon emerged:

> "It's demoralising not feeling like there is hope to get out of this backlog."

> "I'm tired of constantly doing overtime."

And the golden nugget:

> "Wow, you know you're the first senior leader who has asked me how I'm feeling and my opinion of how we can fix this."

Yes, indeed, the draconian leadership that had "led" the business for the previous seven years generally had not asked the team for their opinions on what was wrong. I'll give them the benefit of the doubt and suggest that even the most draconian of leaders/managers must have asked at some point, but the general feeling was that the opinions of the team were unimportant; it was the manager's way or no way. That was an epic failure. Remember, people's perception is their reality. This team's perception was that management was arrogant and did not care about the views of the team or their customers.

One of the best sayings I have heard since becoming a leader resonates well in this regard: *We have two ears and only one mouth for a reason*. In short, they should be used in the same ratio, especially by leaders. Listening to stakeholders is critical, and your own team is a pretty critical stakeholder to be listening to.

> Leaders who don't listen will eventually be
> surrounded by people who have nothing to say.
>
> *-Andy Stanley*

There's only one thing worse than not listening, and that's listening followed by inaction. Off the back of that initial fact-finding mission, I conducted a competency review of the leadership, attempting to get their buy-in to the new way of operating—that is, *every team member's opinion counts*. The intention was to create an environment where the team would enjoy coming to work. In short, rolling out my people-first mantra and mandate to the leaders. A few of the leaders opted out; it wasn't their preferred environment in which to work. They wanted to work in a directive environment. They were loyal to the departed GM, so they chose to do the same, and I'm glad they did. One senior leader I had to wrestle out the door as he clung to the old ways for dear life, white-anting at every opportunity. But then the magic started to happen.

I promoted new leaders into the business and moved a few from my original business unit into this one to act as positive role models and mentors. A series of workshops ensued, getting down to the grassroots of the process and service issues. We trained several team members up in Six Sigma, giving them the licence (albeit within an appropriate change management-controlled environment) to identify low-hanging fruit. Other teams were mobilised to tackle some of the larger issues.

The first breakthrough happened after just two months, with one of the departments achieving service levels, then more in the weeks that followed to the point that by the end of three months, something like 90% of the business unit was in service standards. Now I agree that sounds fanciful, and I wouldn't believe it myself if

I hadn't been part of it, but it was real. Overtime stopped. The vast majority of the 80 people designated for retrenchment were safe. Around 20 people left as the new environment wasn't for them, and that was fine; I appreciated their honesty. We not only achieved the $9 million cost reduction but surpassed it, reaching an $11 million cost reduction. The unit cost of processing transactions had reduced by around 30%, which was a very significant leap towards a profitable business unit.

The most telling metric of all came some nine months after we commenced the turnaround operation. The next team member engagement survey was due, and the results were staggering—the engagement score was, wait for it … 80% (up from 35% the year prior). The item "At work, my opinions count" returned a score of close to 90% when previously it was down around 25%, a staggering result. Never was it so evident to me that putting the team members first made a tangible difference. It was a level playing field in that business unit for the first time in many people's living memory, and they were proud. My visits to the coffee shop each morning to grab my breakfast were no longer met with the sight of team members dragging their feet into the office, like kids returning to school after the summer break. It's no exaggeration to say that heads were held high; there was a spring in their step, and their newfound enjoyment of coming to work was evident for all to see.

A critical measure that I haven't spoken of is customer complaints. These fell to a previously unseen low as well; backlogs didn't exist. The team were happy and this was being reflected in the quality of service they were providing. Needless to say, there were plenty of celebrations of the success we had achieved together. The impossible had become possible because we took the time to listen and then acted.

Now, to be clear, a lot of hard work went into achieving those financial results. The team rose to the challenge. There were countless long days initially, and there were failures along the way, too. But the cool thing was that we all learnt together. I've summarised the fundamentals of that period of change to illustrate the key outcomes as this is a book on people leadership, not process improvement. Importantly, each of the above outcomes was sustained and not a one-hit-wonder.

This is another important by-product of getting the team involved because they then owned the results and took pride in them; it wasn't done to them under sufferance. This was a huge step towards building a truly self-actualizing team overall, something that was previously thought impossible. In fairness, it wasn't even on the radar under the previous regime.

This was a turnaround on a grand scale, but its lessons can be applied no matter the size of your team or business unit. We all want to be valued and feel that our contribution matters. I can't imagine not ever asking my team for their opinions. Naturally, some of you will be reading this and thinking, "Well, in a crisis, there's no time to ask". That's true, and there will always be unique circumstances that will compel you as a leader to take charge in an emergency. If your building's burning down, you don't have time to canvass the views of your team, do you?

But in a general sense, wherever possible, I encourage you to ask your team for their views. Don't do it in a cynical way, assuming you already know the answer. Be honest with them and say, "I think X, what do you think?" Sometimes you may still need to run with your original view, but you'll be amazed at how often a fantastic enhancement to your initial concept will be generated from airing it with the team. To this end, sometimes you are better off not even sharing your original idea as it can restrain the thought process. Instead, be honest about that too:

> "Here's our problem. Now, I do have an idea of what I would like to do to remedy it, but before I share that, I'd love to hear your suggestions."

And don't just involve the team with solving problems. Get them to help shape the plans of your team/business. When the team feel they are truly part of something, they will be inspired to go the extra mile. Naturally, some team members won't want to offer views or maybe even feel like they're not qualified to do so. The reality is everyone notices something or has a view, so as leaders we should try to garner this feedback.

A word of caution: If you seek the views of your team and one or two don't want to play ball—perhaps they're introverts uncomfortable with offering their ideas—it is counterproductive to keep pushing. It can have the unintended consequence of causing disengagement.

In time, these people may well feel comfortable offering their views, but they should never be made to feel uncomfortable for not doing so. Again, we have two ears and one mouth for a reason, so if a team member tells you they're not comfortable speaking up, respect their wishes and move on to those that are.

> If you do not believe that listening to the best
> people in the business telling you what they know
> will help you succeed, then you have allowed your
> ego and arrogance to get the best of you.
>
> *-Andy Albright*

8: CATCH YOUR TEAM DOING THINGS RIGHT

Managers of old were prone to pick fault with their employees' work. After all, it's easy to sit in judgement on your "subordinates", and it was expected, wasn't it? Hopefully, we have moved on from those dark ages and a positive leadership trait to have in your toolkit today is to *catch people doing things right!* A strange saying, yes, because we're used to the negative connotation of catching people out, BUT what a powerful tool it is to encourage your team.

It's a simple coaching/leadership tool whereby you do as the phrase suggests. When someone does something well, you notice and applaud. Importantly, this doesn't just mean an overall achievement. It could be a part of a project or process they have been struggling with. Just as when someone does the wrong thing, and you take them on a bit of a journey to learn why it was wrong (to stop it from happening again), by catching someone doing the right thing and explaining why it was so good, the positive impact will live on in their minds and the act will be repeated.

The most important thing to remember when delivering feedback on areas where someone is doing well (just as when catching people falling short) is to be specific; otherwise, how do they know what was so good about it? So instead of just saying "Good job!" or "Great work!", explain why it was good or great. For example:

"Mary, it was great what you did on that tender process. You came in ahead of all the deadlines you agreed to and were able to create sale volumes 10% higher than we had predicted—well done!"

So, you see, next time Mary goes to work on a tender for you, she will remember the specific feedback you gave her about coming in ahead of deadlines, and there's a strong chance she'll try to replicate the success and, being in sales, who wouldn't want to go higher than the target!

Appreciation can make a day, even change a life. Your willingness to put into words is all that is necessary.

-Margaret Cousins

As part of your repertoire for building a highly engaged culture, make it a habit to look for opportunities each day to encourage your team and catch them doing the right thing. This habit then stands a strong chance of becoming embedded in your work culture. It becomes even more powerful when peers catch each other doing the right thing because it shows they are starting to gain a deep understanding of what success looks like.

9: CELEBRATE SUCCESSES

A natural flow-on from catching people doing the right thing is celebrating the individual and collective things that have gone well. Too often, leaders get swept up in the gloom and doom of things not going so well and communicate only about where their business/department/team needs to improve. But how do your team members recognise what success looks like if you don't celebrate it?

Earlier in the book, we discussed public criticism, and I pointed out that it is rarely, if ever, acceptable. Public praise, however, is a great way to have the efforts of high-performing individuals emulated. A saying I use often is *public praise, private criticism*! In other words, keep your criticism of individuals behind closed doors for the reasons explained earlier, but by all means, shout from the rooftops about the great work of your people and celebrate them.

Be spontaneous with such recognition. For example, if one of your team has done excellent work today, go up to the person and tell them so straightaway—don't wait for the next one-on-one or town hall. If it warrants it, tell the whole team! Importantly, don't just sit on it.

You've caught them doing something great, so tell them.

> The deepest principle in human nature is the
> craving to be appreciated.
>
> *-William James*

Additionally, in the communications forum that we spoke of earlier, find a way to weave in a recap of all the great things that have happened and celebrate them. You could mark the occasion with morning tea, after-work drinks, or a tangible gift. Often, the recognition in front of peers is a sufficient reward, but don't be shy to give someone a gift for truly excellent work. You'll be surprised at the effect.

The important thing to bear in mind with this is that you're setting a precedent. Be careful about that, or you may end up causing disengagement amongst others later. For example, if someone achieves a sales target or other significant milestone, be sure to explain precisely why you are rewarding them:

> "Congratulations, Joe—for being the first person to
> ever achieve $10,000 in sales within a month,
> you're receiving a weekend away on us."

Next time the bar gets raised, who knows, there might be another random reward!

There's a balancing act with reward and recognition programs, often the go-to approach for rewarding individuals. If you don't get the balance right, they will become like wallpaper—there but no longer noticed, just part of the background. People expect them and become cynical about them: "Whose turn is it to be employee of the month this month?" kind of thing. I encourage a blend of regular, consistent rewards for defined achievements that, if no one achieves them, do not get awarded, and ad-hoc ones to mix things up.

As I mentioned above, celebrating successes is not just about handing out monetary or other tangible rewards. The higher intent here is to have a culture wherein great work is celebrated and replicated. It might even spur on the less engaged.

Sometimes leaders think they have to establish an expensive reward and recognition program and end up getting themselves mired in detail. *Don't let perfect be the enemy of good.* And if funds are tight, just a simple public thank you to the team members who have done outstanding work may well suffice.

If you can implement a reward program of sorts, it's worth asking your team how they would like to be rewarded. Find out what works for them and your business. There's no one-size-fits-all, and remember, reward programs don't need to cost a fortune. Even just presenting those cheap, readily available trophies is a fun way of rewarding success. The most important thing is to do something to celebrate great work. ***Success breeds success***.

10: EMPOWER

Earlier, we discussed micromanagement and the dire effect it has on team engagement. As highlighted then, there is a time and a place for close management of your team members as it's the responsibility of a leader to ensure that the work is getting done correctly. However, this is about having appropriate training and guidance for the team members right from the very beginning of their time with you as a new employee and as they develop. When a new team member starts, or when they're learning new things, you may have to oversee the work they do. Arguably, it's reckless not to. A micromanager, however, will continue to check up on these people long after they need it. A leader who empowers their team would instead "check in". There's a big difference. Consider these different approaches:

A. If I am "checking up", my words would be, "John, have you completed steps A, B, C, D and E? Are you going to do F, G and H next?"

B. If I am "checking in", I would say something like, "How are you going, John? Are you comfortable that you're across all of the steps? Is there anything I can help with?"

When we empower our people, not only do they grow personally and professionally, they also tend to own whatever it is they're being tasked to deliver and ultimately, they become engaged. There will, of course, be varying degrees of engagement, and not everyone will become engaged to the same level. So you're going to set yourself up for a fall if you expect everyone to hit those top levels of engagement. However, I would take an 80% engagement level over a 30–40% engagement level any day of the week. By empowering your people, you are setting them and yourself up for success.

> It's not the tools you have faith in. Tools are just tools, they work, or they don't work. It's the people you have faith in or not.
>
> *-Steve Jobs*

Consider when you were learning to ride a bike, or more recently perhaps, teaching a child to. Initially, there are the training wheels, and as the child gets used to the concept of balance and starts to gain confidence, you might raise one wheel slightly higher off the ground; you might remove one altogether as the child's confidence grows. The child might progress to having you gently hold the back of the bike with them pedalling. They'll fall a couple of times (hopefully, you're doing it on grass!) before suddenly they nail it and ride confidently. They'll still fall from time to time, hence the helmet.

This is a good analogy for empowerment. The training wheels and your holding the back of the bike are the "guard rails"; the safety net, if you like. They ensure that while learning, there is virtually no chance of injury—much like when you're training people on tasks, you might have a 100% check rate to prevent "injury" to the recipient of your service. Once the safety wheels come off, there's a higher risk of injury. But this risk is mitigated by the child now knowing what they're doing. You weigh up that risk and put in place the guard rail of the helmet so that if the child does come off the bike, the most vulnerable area is protected. Bringing this back to a work scenario, the "safety helmet" could be a random sample of the person's work by peers or some other checkpoint, but what it isn't is having you standing there holding onto the back of their bike to stop them from falling off. Now, imagine what it would be like if your child had you always holding onto the back of their bike or they always had the training wheels on—*how much longer would it take them to gain the confidence to ride independently?* Once your team members are comfortable with the tasks set—and by that, I mean they feel competent and confident—empowering them is about setting them targets and creating guard rails for them to operate within safely. When you check in with your team, you'll understand where they're up to and have the opportunity to redirect if needs be. An empowered and engaged team is more likely to self-actualize. If you set a target of processing 100 widgets in a day, they'll strive for that and even try to beat it. If you micromanage and check up on them in units below that, that's the parameter they're working within—for example, "Do this widget, OK ... now this one, now this ... wow, you're up to three." That would make for a long day!

The above is a generalisation, of course. There will be exceptions on both sides. I am purely speaking from experience because, as I mentioned earlier, I have sadly worked with someone of that micromanagement ilk. The trick to empowerment is nailing those guard rails and your risk tolerance. There will be some industries that require much tighter tolerances, whereas others can be quite liberal. It will all depend on your risk appetite versus the rewards that can be gained by letting your team do what they do best. To ever so slightly paraphrase Roosevelt:

> The best executive is the one who has sense
> enough to pick good people to do what they want
> done, and self-restraint enough to keep from
> meddling with them while they do it.[3]
>
> *-Theodore Roosevelt*

---

[3]   Slight tweaking to bring it into the gender-inclusive 21st century.

I spoke earlier about the Financial Services business where there was a seismic uplift in people engagement. Part of that success was through listening to and empowering them with such tools as Six Sigma. They then went hunting of their own accord for opportunities to improve processes, though always supported by change controls—the guard rails.

Let's drill into the benefits of self-actualization for a moment longer. It builds engagement through empowerment and it prevents you from smothering your team in a blanket of micromanagement. Spoon-feeding your team every step of the way means they won't know what to do when you're not around. Indeed, there's a risk of the team being so accustomed to being told what to do next, and checked up on, that they have no inclination (or frankly, ability) to take control and think for themselves should you or other leaders not happen to be there because you have taken a well-earned break. Again, appropriate guard rails provide the framework for balanced work and home lives—something that we should all be craving if we're not already!

We all need to be able to step away from the business from time to time and put the tools down. If you're a micromanager, how do you do that? If you find yourselves having to micromanage despite having the above frameworks in place, it's worth asking yourself if you have the right people. If you find yourself micromanaging because that's what your manager expects of you (and you are being micromanaged yourself), it's time for you to have a difficult conversation with your manager. What is causing the trust deficit? How can you give your manager the confidence not to micromanage you? Can you show your manager what success looks like? Being a successful leader is not just about managing our team(s); it's about managing up the line too.

Empowerment is all about trust at the end of the day; therefore, build a training system that you trust. Set up guard rails that you trust. Have recruitment and selection processes in place that you trust. Train your people and trust them to do what they're paid to do.

11: DELEGATE, DON'T ABDICATE

Following on from the empowering of your team, one of the best gifts you can give your team and yourself is the art of delegation. To many, this is a tricky one, but if you've mastered the art of empowering your team, it goes hand in hand with it. A well-developed and empowered team will be capable of absorbing more complex tasks, and you will therefore be able to delegate to them. Sounds simple, and ultimately it is, but what this doesn't mean is freeing you up so you can kick back and relax. As you would expect, this would cause resentment amongst your team. No, it is about selectively delegating tasks that are second nature to you, but that might be a stretch for your team; in turn, this frees you up to work on more complex tasks and develop yourself. It's a cycle!

What delegating isn't is abdication. Remember, you are still accountable for the work, but you are handing over responsibility to one of your team to complete the work on your behalf.

> Delegation is the most important style of leadership, if you can't delegate then you are not a leader.
>
> *Harold Zulu*

The steps to follow for delegation are much the same as those for empowering your team. You want to set your team members up for success, so you choose the right person and the right time. Call me old school, but keep an eye on symbolism here as well. Don't be THAT person who delegates a bunch of their work so they can leave on time while the proud delegates who have the honour of doing your work have to work extended hours. This may mean having to think laterally for a cascading approach—that is, perhaps the person to whom you want to delegate this task is already snowed under, and you don't want to break them. So consider whether another team member might learn from the opportunity of doing some of that person's work, which in turn will free them up. That cycle again!

Remember the training wheels on the child's bike analogy and create a safe environment for your team to have the opportunity to do some of your tasks with "guard rails". Provide lots of coaching, but don't smother your team members. Be left of centre with what you delegate, don't just stick to tasks. You could ask them to attend certain meetings on your behalf, in this way exposing them to a different set of people in the organisation and a different environment.

By delegating appropriately, you are affording your team the opportunity for personal growth and will reap the reward in the form of your own development. We should never be too busy to learn.

There will always be some members of your team who are more ready to have complex tasks delegated than others. This is natural as everyone is at different stages of their development journey. By refining this talent and identifying one or two members of your team who could undertake your entire role after a series of successful delegations over time, you are honing the development of ready-made successors to yourself. Some people hesitate to do this because they fear looking dispensable. I believe that is short-sighted. Consider the opposite. If you have ready-made successors, it means you could be seen as ready for your next opportunity, and in the meantime, you'll have the upside of being able to take a break knowing that the business is in safe hands. And that's got to be a good thing. Right?

> As much as you need a strong personality to build a
> business from scratch, you also must understand
> the art of delegation. I have to be good at helping
> people run the individual businesses, and I have to
> be willing to step back. The company must be set
> up so it can continue without me.
>
> -Sir Richard Branson

Larger organisations tend to have embedded processes for ongoing delegations of authorities. These set out the various financial/operational decisions that can be made by certain individuals within the business. For example, on the financial side, it might permit a team leader to authorise payments to customers of up to $5,000, and anything between $5,000 and $20,000 might need the sign off of a manager; payments above $20,000 require the next level of manager up etc. Having such delegated authority registers in place ensures there is no misunderstanding around what each member of the team is empowered to do. Some organisations then permit their managers to further delegate within the framework in particular circumstances (such as when going on leave).

For example, if you have signing authority for payments between $5,000 and $20,000 and happen to go on leave without delegating your authority, your team members will need to go to the next level manager for authorisation—no doubt, the senior manager will soon tire of this. So, you temporarily delegate your authority to the next most senior person in your team, who has demonstrated they can be trusted. Remember, you're delegating, not abdicating. To many, having increased delegations is seen as a reward.

Equally, it can act as a demotivator should authorities be taken away.

If you operate within a small to medium business, you should consider having a simple delegated-authority register. (I'll work on the assumption that if you're working in a large organisation, this will already be in place, but most certainly, if you don't have one, you should!) It really does help make it very clear who is responsible for what. Additionally, it serves as a control, meaning files can be reviewed in your regular audits and processes tested to ensure that only those people named in the register have authorised the payments. Formula One cars have enormous brakes. Do they have these so they can drive slowly? No, they have them so they can drive faster! The same goes for controls.

A well-thought-out and structured delegated-authority register will enable you to articulate who is responsible and accountable for what in your team or organisation, not to slow things down but speed things up. Progression across the matrix with increased authorities over time as experience is broadened and results delivered will serve as a means to develop and recognise your people as well. Additionally, it is a much more structured approach to delegating authorities, which, if done well, is easily understood by all parties.

12: HOLD REGULAR ONE-ON-ONES

Regardless of the size of your organisation or how long you've been a leader, staying connected to your team members is critical. Aside from anything else, you will understand how they're performing more deeply by engaging in regular communication with them.

As I have said before, we have two ears and only one mouth for a reason, so listening more than talking is the key.

> Most people do not listen with the intent to understand; they listen with the intent to reply.
>
> *-Stephen R. Covey, Leadership First*

Creating a regular one-on-one forum with each of your direct reports is a terrific way of formally staying connected. Ad-hoc interactions throughout the working week will enhance these formal meetings.

I tend to work on a ratio of my direct reports doing at least 60% of the talking in these discussions. It's not about me lecturing them, but them telling me how they're going, what hurdles they are facing, what they have achieved (hopefully, I've noticed), what they're planning, and what additional training may be required.

Naturally, it is an opportunity for me to redirect also. I tend to have my team members set the agenda and then ask for their permission to add things to it—in terms of ownership, I openly declare these meetings to be their meetings, not mine.

There's no set rule or idea as to the frequency of these discussions. The more important thing is that they're regular—so hold them weekly, fortnightly, or monthly. You might decide to adjust the frequency depending upon the experience of the person or the criticality of information flow with that person. For example, if you lead a team of data entry administrators, weekly one-on-one discussions is perhaps overkill. However, if salespeople report to you, weekly meetings could be advisable.

How you frame these meetings also matters. Remember the difference between checking in (which is what these should be) and checking up (which is what these meetings shouldn't be—unless there are performance issues, which is a separate matter). Consider asking open-ended questions during the discussions to elicit as much feedback as possible and thereby help you to help your team. For example:

> "Since we last met, what has worked well for you,
> and where have things not gone so well?"

You might also like to set some developmental tasks for them and check in to see how they've gone with them.

As I mentioned above, you should add to the dialogue with your team members by regularly finding a reason to interact with them between one-on-one sessions. Don't fall into the trap of simply deferring all discussions with your team to their next one-on-one; deal with urgent matters straightaway. But equally, don't be afraid to push non-urgent matters that arise between these meetings to the next one. Find the rhythm that works for you and your team members. Importantly, these don't need to be lengthy discussions either. If you can nail the agenda in half an hour, that's great. Be fluid. As with everything in life, it's about balance. Sometimes you might need extra time.

I've spoken before about authenticity. It's critical in all areas of leadership, but nowhere is it more so than in your deep conversations with each of your team members. You need to trust them, and guess what? That works both ways because they want and need to trust you too. By conducting these sessions well, you have the opportunity to build a strong connection with each of your team members. That in itself will help drive up your engagement levels.

We've concentrated on your direct reports for the purpose of one-on-ones, but what about those of you who are running large departments or divisions, or you're a small to medium-sized business that has several layers of management for various reasons. How do you stay connected with the team members who report to your direct reports?

Well, firstly, you should set the expectation with your direct reports that they will conduct these sessions with *their* direct reports. Nothing speaks louder than setting an example—that is, if you ask your direct reports to have such discussions with their direct reports when they never have them with you, they're going to see you as a hypocrite!

Secondly, you can take the opportunity to host some "skip level" discussions; essentially, chats between yourself and the team members who report to your direct reports. These are usually irregular in frequency (or you may choose to set a frequency; it's entirely up to you). The agenda will tend to be much more high level and will, of course, vary depending on the nature of your business. Their higher intent is to reassure you that the culture is what it should be (or give you a heads-up if it isn't). Are your messages getting through, and what do you *need* to hear (not *want*)? I find these discussions incredibly powerful, and the better your workplace culture, the more powerful these sessions will be.

By building trust with your wider team, you will have a wide network of team members ready to tell you, like I said, what you need to hear.

The more your team members trust you, the more candid these discussions will be. On occasion, you may be unpleasantly surprised with what they tell you are issues at their level in the business. Be grateful to them for doing so because if you didn't have the culture you have to elicit this feedback, the matter might well have gone underground, causing a more serious issue later on.

Finally, whether it's a one-on-one with a direct report or a skip-level discussion, the other very important things to remember are:

1. If the person you are holding the discussion with tells you something in confidence, it must remain so. That's just plain integrity, and although it's obvious, it's well worth pointing out. If you think you have a good reason to pass it on, you must ask their permission and abide by their refusal. If there comes a time when the feedback *must* be passed on (for legal reasons, for example), show some courtesy and let the person know first.

2. Again, although obvious (believe me when I say that many get it wrong), if you commit to an action item, do it (just as you would expect from your team). If, for any reason, you haven't been able to, tell your team this. We've all been there, I'm sure, where our managers have promised something and then either been too busy and so didn't do it or, worse, just didn't bother because they thought we'd forget. Guess what? We don't forget! As the saying goes, actions speak louder than words. It's incredibly powerful to do what you say you're going to do. It shows you care, and it shows that the team member whom you promised to follow something up for is important.

13: NEVER SHIRK THE PERFORMANCE REVIEW

A critical tool in every leader's toolkit is the performance review, mainly because it draws a line in the sand of how an individual is performing relative to their KPIs. It would be rare to work in a large organisation that did not have a performance appraisal process. I have worked for organisations that hold these quarterly (possibly too frequently), but most have them set half-yearly with an annual summary to assess performance across the year.

If you're working for a smaller business (or your own business) and you don't have a performance appraisal process, I highly recommend that you implement one. While large organisations have set formats and the documentation can be rather complex, they don't need to be. A simple form that highlights the KPIs/objectives that are in place for everyone, together with a measurement against your business's values (more on this below), is all that is required. Importantly, for the KPI measurement section, you should ensure consistency by providing a range of achievements. The usual ones are "Meets Expectations", "Exceeds Expectations", "Outstanding", as well as in the other direction: "Improvement Needed" or "Unacceptable".

Every large organisation has a method they use for performance reviews. Some use bell curves where they only want a certain percentage of employees rated in each rating type (e.g. Meeting Expectations, Exceeding Expectations or Outstanding Overall). This means they have calibration meetings to ensure each manager has rated their team members consistently—often horse-trading goes on in these discussions, bumping people's ratings up while others get bumped down. An even harsher approach is forced ranking, which takes the bell curve one step further and imposes hard cut-offs, and individuals have their ratings ranked accordingly.

Both the above methods make for quite challenging performance reviews because, as calibration has not yet occurred, you have to hold the discussion without knowing the team member's rating. I am not a fan of either method, and I won't labour the merits or otherwise here because each organisation will have their own unique approach. I believe the performance discussion should be allowed to flow naturally between the team member and their leader. Any rankings can then be used outside of that to determine bonuses or pay increases. For the purpose of discussing getting the best out of performance reviews, let's assume no such systems are in place. If your organisation already has them, you'll need to adapt accordingly.

> A Performance Appraisal that is conducted effectively leads to greater employee morale, higher productivity, creating a positive culture and improved overall performance and effectiveness of an organisation.
>
> -Kumar Parakala

Like one-on-ones, I believe the ratio of talking and listening should be 60/40, meaning the team member under review should do at least 60% of the talking. With this in mind, I have a personal approach to these whereby I won't book a time for the discussion itself until the team member has submitted their self-assessment of results versus KPIs, as well as how they have performed against the values. I do this because it is critical that everyone gives serious thought to their own performance, just like I will in evaluating how they've gone.

To this end, I always lead off a performance review discussion by asking the person how they feel they have gone in the review period relative to their KPIs and organisational values. In addition, I ask them two simple questions:

"Where do you feel you have excelled?"

"Upon reflection, how could you have improved or done things differently for better results during the period?"

As they talk, I make extensive notes to help me later in writing my review. I encourage those I mentor in leading effective performance reviews to only come into a review discussion with handwritten notes (potentially old school!), my logic being symbolism. If you come in with typewritten notes, it creates an impression that you've made up your mind already (a bit like a school report card), and no correspondence shall be entered into—more on this later.

My golden rule for an effective performance review is that there should be **no surprises**. In fact, if you take nothing else away from this section but this one element, that's cool because springing a surprise on a hapless team member is one of the worst habits, I've seen leaders exhibit over the years. You may have been here yourself. You've gone through the previous six months in the belief you've nailed it. You've hit your KPIs, and you believe you live the company's values, only to attend your performance review and find out that you have these two to three areas where your performance isn't where it should be, and you're not quite living one of the values—SURPRISE! Well, I'd regard that as an epic failure by your leader! If you weren't told you were doing something wrong, how were you supposed to fix it?

As your team member reports on how they feel they have gone, you give your reflections. Do you agree or not? Realistically, because there are no surprises, a performance review should be a summary of all the terrific one-on-ones you've been holding throughout the year—in fact, these can be used as reference tools for the review, particularly for areas where performance hasn't been to the required standard. "Remember, we discussed in our last four one-on-ones your need to focus on improving productivity" kind of thing. The same goes for an individual's particular strengths.

You can reference these to reinforce the message:

> "Mary, a constant theme of our one-on-ones has been your excellent customer service and the accolades you receive from your clients and peers alike. You have nailed this KPI."

It is extremely powerful in these discussions to use as many examples as possible to bring the feedback to life and to reinforce your positive feedback as well as your constructive developmental feedback.

Work your way systematically through each of the KPIs and values, assuming the values are also part of your format; frankly, if they're not, they should be. We've all worked with people who were top performers against KPIs but were like wrecking balls to work with, and that's why many organisations introduced the concept of measuring performance against values too. I have performance managed out of an organisation someone who nailed their KPIs but were abrasive to work with—left unchecked, the person would have been like a termite to the department's culture.

A key part of the performance review is discussing the development plan. In fact, you might find it beneficial to break up the review into two parts and hold the development or training plan on a different day. I tend to do them together (remembering there are no surprises, so any performance or training gaps should be known before this discussion). Again, ask the team member to lead this part of the discussion. You should now address any performance or training gaps by creating some tangible development actions for addressing in the next review period— ideally, no more than three to four, or the list becomes unwieldy and won't get done. If you have someone who has nailed all of their KPIs and are the model team member in terms of the values, then the focus for development may be on further honing a strength or undertaking a special project or different work to build new skills. Everyone has room for growth. So, when you ask the question "What do you see as areas for development?", don't give the person a free pass by agreeing no training is required, even if you have just finished agreeing that they exemplify everything great about a team member. Try new things. Explore what their next role looks like and how they can start preparing for it.

As part of my review process, I have always taken the opportunity to ask my team members to discuss my performance (again, a regular feature of one-on-ones, so the no-surprises policy works in this direction also). Ahead of the review, I ask that they come prepared to discuss the areas where they perceive I am doing well and where I can improve—I don't go so far as having them complete a form; it's more about the quality of the discussion. I find these discussions incredibly beneficial. After all, they live within the leadership shadow I cast every day, so they can provide me with rich learning material from which to improve, material that my own manager doesn't see.

A word of caution with this one. I recommend holding off until you have built up trust credits with your team, so they feel comfortable being completely honest with you (the same goes, of course, with your one-on-one discussions, which are ultimately the conduit to this discussion). Without trust, they will fear the repercussions of being too honest with you or, worse still, just sugar-coat everything and tell you you're perfect, so nothing has been gained. *Another tip here*: only make this part of your performance review process if you are prepared to act on the feedback. Being defensive or dismissive will make the team member regret putting in the effort. Embrace the feedback and treat it as a gift!

You've now completed the review discussion, and it's time to type it all up. This is where the notes you took when listening intently to your team member's self-assessment come in handy. From my experience, nothing is more powerful than using their own words/language in the written review.

They resonate well, and it's easier for them to own what they have articulated. For example, during your discussion with your team member Mary, she told you that she lets herself down with her attention to detail (or lack thereof). This is how I would type that:

> "Mary's productivity has continued to increase throughout the review period, and she feels this will be further enhanced by her continuing to focus on improving her attention to detail, which she believes at times has let her down. I agree with her that this should be an area of focus in the next review period."

Reviews should be about balanced feedback, and how they're written up can make or break their effectiveness. Avoid using words like "but" and "however" (the same goes for the actual discussion itself, of course!) because all people will remember is the negativity that comes next. Stick with the neutral "and" as in the above example.

Consider the change in tone in the example below when "however" has been used instead:

> "Mary's productivity has continued to increase throughout the review period. **However**, to be more effective in this area, she needs to focus on improving her attention to detail, which she believes at times has let her down."

You can see that the "however" has neutralised the positive feedback of the first sentence.

Something to also bear in mind, and it's a pet peeve of mine, is that you should be able to cover over the ratings of a performance review and accurately guess what they are from reading the comments. A trap some people fall into is to rate people low—for example, "Needs improvement"—but then gloss over this with the commentary. Or describe someone as "Outstanding" in their rating and then have neutral commentary that offers no clue as to why they have been rated outstanding. In short, much like the review discussion itself, the richer the commentary by way of tangible examples, the more meaningful the outcome of the review. I like to think of these as standalone documents that tell a story. Anyone should be able to pick up the form, read it and have a deep understanding of the performance of the individual it's discussing.

To this end, particularly in large organisations when doing internal recruitment, I have always asked the candidates for their permission to see their last few reviews as a basis for a reference check. If anything is unclear still, I'll make a call to clarify, but I see them as hugely useful in this regard.

> Done right, a performance review is one of the best opportunities to encourage and support high performers and constructively improve your middle and lower tier workers.
>
> -Kathryn Minshew, AZ Quotes

Like everything in life, we only get out of something what we put into it. A lot of people get hung up on the process, and, yes, I've put a lot of emphasis on how to type up the performance review forms, but the most important aspect of the review is the discussion and the agreed development actions. Both the reviewer and reviewee should be in the right frame of mind for the discussion. They should not be defensive. They should be transparent, honest, and ready to receive feedback. Don't be afraid to postpone a review if you feel that one of you isn't in the right headspace for it. A performance review done well will aid an

individual's progression; one done badly can cause
disengagement.

I mentioned earlier that I am not a fan of calibration sessions and
the whole bell curve approach to ratings, and well, I am not. But
there is a critical need for consistency in applying ratings. It is
crucial to the integrity of the performance review framework that
you apply your ratings equitably—that is, if two people achieve
the same results, it would be unfair to rate one as "Exceeds
Expectations" and the other as "Meets Expectations", unless, of
course, the first person was new to the role and the other a
veteran. But as a general rule you would aim not to have this sort
of discrepancy.

Finally, as should be clear by now, the most important part of the
review is the discussion and the actions that derive from it. Many
organisations use this process to differentiate between employees
for remuneration reviews and bonuses; they are, of course, useful
in this regard. To my mind, however, the performance review (as a
summary of all the previous one-on-one discussions) is a gateway
to what actions will be required in the next review period to
ensure the team member meets performance objectives and
receives the required training. To this end, I encourage using the
development plan as one of the ongoing agenda items at future

one-on-ones. In this way, you and the team member can address the actions and ensure development continues to occur.

14: OFFER EVERYONE A CAREER PATH

While not everyone wants to be the next CEO, a large proportion of any organisation wants to see that they have a future with that business and can progress. Therefore, mapping out indicative career paths can be a way of retaining team members and building engagement.

Once upon a time, people regarded progression in an organisation to be vertical and felt compelled to rise through the "ranks" of leadership as high as they could go. While, for many, that remains their aspiration, this has tended to evolve over time with a focus instead on the breadth of roles, meaning that sideways moves are just as critical in terms of career progression as vertical ones. Every organisation and every industry is different in this regard.

> I want to look back on my career and be proud of
> the work, and be proud that I tried everything.
>
> *-Jon Stewart*

We spoke of development plans earlier when discussing performance reviews and the next logical evolution to these is career plans. These career discussions don't need to occur with the same frequency as performance reviews or development plans; once a year is sufficient, and they are all interlinked. For example, if someone has an aspiration to learn a new role as part of their career plan, there's no reason not to incorporate the building blocks to this in their development plan; the two are not mutually exclusive. I encourage a three-year horizon for career plans. These plans should consider the key steps and extracurricular activities required to help the team member realise their aspiration. Like development plans, they should be tangible and measurable. Specific development needs or work experience should all be articulated and mapped out. It won't be perfect, but it will act as a guide.

I like to incorporate some "try before you buy" activities into the plans for the team. For example, if someone wants to learn how to do a completely different role in your business, give them the opportunity to do some work experience alongside a subject-matter expert over a set period. It's hugely empowering. The team member feels supported in their aspirations, and they get a taste of what it is like to undertake that role before committing to it. Assuming they do commit to it, it also gives them a degree of training before moving across into the role permanently.

In days gone by, I have seen organisations rate individuals on what they consider to be their potential. I've seen this be a transparent process and one that is done behind the scenes in a "Talent Review". Interestingly, many organisations undertake these reviews in a vault-like manner, with the results unable to be shared unless you happen to be one of the stars of the business regarded as "top talent". My feeling is that this is wrong. While most of these reviews do use two lenses—actual performance in current role and future potential—the future potential is highly subjective and done in isolation from the individual. For example, if someone's performance wasn't that great in a particular year because of environmental factors or they weren't enjoying their role, is it fair that this person is then tarred with the brush of "no potential"? Remember, people live up to or down to our expectations, so if someone happens to find themselves pigeonholed in that way, are they ever going to break free of that perception? For this reason, I believe in transparency. We should have very open and honest discussions with our team members about their careers, of which their potential is, of course, a critical element.

If your manager doesn't believe you have a bright future with the business, shouldn't you have a right of reply with either the opportunity to demonstrate you are better than they think you or the opportunity to move to another role more suited to your capabilities?

The advantage of transparent discussions about careers is that everyone knows where they stand and can do something about it.

Maybe the perceived lack of progression of the individual has been a blind spot to the person and a simple tweak to their performance/demeanour could overcome the problem? Maybe they need to hear that, in your opinion, they cannot yet reach the dizzy heights of management—because it's just that, *your opinion*. At least by hearing the feedback, they can act on it. This might mean adjusting their behaviour because they're now aware of what has created the perception—importantly, *they now know*. By being transparent, team members who are not deemed suitable for progression can also make a choice. If they're never going to get an opportunity to progress for whatever reason, they may elect to leave; that's also fine because they may thrive somewhere else.

Such conversations can be confronting, but isn't it better that they're had openly rather than behind the team member's back? Positives can then come off it, and it really does then demonstrate you are a transparent leader.

As part of a people-focused, engaged culture, it's also beneficial to communicate with the team when people undertake intra-business role movements. This is always important but especially so in large businesses so that team members can hear of a colleague's progress. It reinforces the value placed on career progression within the organisation. It's hugely empowering for the team to witness the success of their peers and the worth of the career plan process. If it can happen to a colleague, it can happen to them too. The business they are part of is truly investing in their talent, including them. What a boost that is to engagement levels!

15: PAY PEOPLE WHAT THEY'RE WORTH

If you're a junior to middle-level leader of a medium or large organisation, you could be forgiven for thinking you have no influence on the pay levels of your team members. Generally, there are overarching remuneration philosophies in place. However, you still have a role to play. If you are a senior leader in such an organisation or indeed the owner of one, you most definitely have a role to play.

While everyone is different, how we are remunerated, whether we like it or not, is a significant hygiene factor that affects our level of engagement. If a team member, regardless of their level in the organisation, feels they are not being paid what they're worth, even the most engaged performer will eventually let this affect their performance. Despite business policies that tend to prohibit the sharing of such information, a lot of people are all too transparent with what they get paid. So, if you are paying someone a lot less for doing the same work as their peers, firstly, you're not being fair (unless there are extenuating circumstances), and secondly, they will most likely find out!

As well as your team knowing what they each get paid, if they have dared to look beyond the walls of your business to the market, they may well also know they can get paid more elsewhere.

Depending upon your jurisdiction, there are awards/safety nets for many industries to ensure employees are paid appropriately. These minimum standards are set by law and must be adhered to. Different industries will, of course, have varying levels of demand for employees. Regardless, if you want your team to support you and be passionate about coming to work every day, pay them appropriately so that the hygiene factor is removed. Appropriate pay is an important ingredient in being an *employer of choice*. If your team members know you are fair, and the overall organisation is too, they may not even look elsewhere to beat their salary.

This is where, even as a junior or middle-level leader, you have a role to play. If someone on your team is not being remunerated fairly, I would argue you have an obligation to them and the business to speak up and try to fix the matter before it becomes a serious issue. Show some genuine care for your team member.

If you wait until your team member comes to you with a resignation letter because they've been offered more money elsewhere, it's too late. Yes, you can always counteroffer, and yes, you may be successful on some occasions, but frankly, that's an engagement killer. Most people will quite rightly ask themselves, or you, why they weren't paid fairly/appropriately in the first place. Why did it take their resignation for them to have their pay adjusted? That's a fair question. Wearing your empathetic leader hat, do you think it would be powerful for you to intervene to ensure your valued team member has their pay adjusted to an appropriate level before they have to say anything? I would say yes. That would be a great indicator of genuine people-first leadership. Naturally, the remuneration levels must be balanced with affordability and profits, but attempting to save a few dollars on the bottom line here can be counterproductive.

Consider this: you have a team member who is paid $80,000 per year, but the market is paying a minimum of $85,000; this person gets headhunted by a competitor organisation and eventually accepts their offer of employment of $87,500. Now, you have to replace the position and, of course, you can't find anyone for less than $85,000 because that's what the market is paying. On top of that salary, you will most likely have to pay a recruitment agency around 12% of the salary package as their fee—so another $10,200. So you're now up to $95,200 annualised before you take into consideration the other costs of turnover that are outlined earlier in the book, including training and lost opportunity costs (remembering that turnover costs can range from 50 to 150% of the departing person's salary). Had you simply paid the employee what the market is paying (i.e. $85,000, as a minimum), you would have saved your business a minimum of $10,200 (being the recruitment fee) but most likely somewhere between $40,000 and $120,000 (being the stated 50–150% turnover cost range). Not to mention the fact you would have also prevented experience from walking out the door. If you extrapolate this over a number of team members throughout the year, it soon adds up.

In summary, with a people-centric approach, ensure your team members are remunerated appropriately and remove that potential objection/distraction. If your team know they're being paid fairly, this won't be a consideration for them, and they'll be focused on your customers, not the missing dollars from their pay!

SOME FINAL THOUGHTS TO HELP YOU BUILD ENGAGEMENT

ENCOURAGE WORK–LIFE BALANCE

As this suggests, there should be a balance between the two. In fact, a better way of positioning this is "life–work balance" as surely life should come first!

Earlier, I outlined an example of my assuming that the long days a talented team member worked were detrimental to her. In that instance, I was wrong. Nonetheless, as a leader, it is your responsibility to create the right environment where your team focus on results and don't think it a badge of honour to work long hours.

If you watch the clock, so will your team, and unless your business is about making timepieces, is that really important for you? I suspect not. Remember, a burnt-out team is not an engaged team, and a non-engaged team is a less productive one. As we've discussed earlier, there are always times when extra hours are required; a highly engaged team will volunteer this: *don't take advantage!*

CARE. YES, TRULY GIVE A DAMN

You can't be expected to know and be involved in every aspect of your team's lives, and frankly, that's probably not even appropriate. But everyone has stuff they are dealing with outside of work, so when those life-defining moments occur, demonstrate you care.

Caring, of course, goes hand in hand with empathy and compassion, which we discussed earlier. When you have high-performing team members who are always going the extra mile for you, and something has happened in their personal life (whether bad news or great news), take an interest and act accordingly. For example, how powerful would it be if, unasked, you offered one of your team members, whose child was about to graduate from school, the afternoon off to see the ceremony? Or you have noticed a team member has been putting in longer hours consistently of late to ensure an important project can hit its milestones, so you offer them a day off to recharge, on you! These are the one-percenters that really do make a positive difference to your work environment and help create that highly engaged workplace you're seeking!

CREATE SAFE OPPORTUNITIES FOR FEEDBACK FROM YOUR TEAM

All feedback is a gift, so create opportunities to receive that gift openly. Remember that, although it can be confronting, the fact that your team members dare to give you feedback means they trust you.

> One of the most sincere forms of respect is actually listening to what another has to say.
>
> *-Bryant McGill*

Don't betray that trust. Once it's gone, it's gone. Use the feedback wisely, and be sure to loop back to whoever gave the feedback to let them know what you've done about it. That will demonstrate not only that you took it seriously but that you also genuinely appreciated them taking the time to pass it on.

BE PRESENT

As a leader, regardless of your level, you have a million things going on in your day and not enough time to do it all. But when you have personal time with your team members, whether it's a one-on-one, a performance review, or a casual drop-by, they deserve to have your undivided focus. Aside from it being bad manners to check your emails or phone messages when you're with another person, it can make them think they're unimportant to you. They're not. Well, at least they shouldn't be!

A quick side story involving a leader I worked with who shares many of the characteristics featured in my poor traits of leadership examples: I was doing a career discussion with him and one of the senior team members. During this meeting, he repeatedly yawned and checked his emails and was blatantly rude during one of the most critical conversations you can have with a team member, let alone someone who was such an asset to the business. It was so bad that I weaved into the conversation that "Sue" was well equipped to fly to the moon, and he nodded—yes, regrettably she had noticed how rude he was, and yes, I called out the behaviour with him.

In short. **Be present!**

STEP AWAY FROM YOUR OFFICE

Get out and about amongst your team; don't hide in your office or behind your desk. And by this, I'm not referring to the outdated management philosophy called "management by walking around", which was a bit like how a teacher walks around their classroom to make sure the children are working. No, this isn't that!

Believe it or not, your team want to see you. The more you're out amongst it all, sparking up a conversation and checking in (again, not checking up!), the more likely your team will view you as approachable and speak up when there's an issue. More importantly, they'll embrace you as part of the team, not just someone aloof and sitting in an office all day, *as long as your behaviours match, of course!*

BE SELF-AWARE

Remember how you wanted to be treated before you hit the dizzy heights of management? Do unto others and all that! This is fairly straightforward and is again related to empathy. Before you were in a management position, remember the days when you were critical of the leaders you worked for and with—the behaviours you didn't like, quite possibly emanating from many of the poor traits outlined earlier? If you take nothing else away from this book, use how you felt in those moments of being treated poorly to stop yourself from treating others that same way. Instead, channel the buzz you experienced when treated well and pay that forward.

Be aware of the shadow you're casting. How is your mood manifesting to your team? As a leader, the spotlight is on you. Be mindful of your actions and the reactions they cause.

> Become the leader that people would follow
> voluntarily, even if you had no title or position.
>
> *-Brian Tracy*

Leading people is a privilege, we all have an opportunity to create an environment where every day is a great day to come to work.

-Alexander N.
Andrews

BE A BETTER PEOPLE LEADER TODAY
THAN YOU WERE YESTERDAY!
UNLIKE A BOSS.

Made in the USA
Las Vegas, NV
11 December 2022

61848622R00092